rac

First aid for your car

Your expert guide to common problems & how to fix them

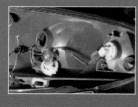

Carl Collins

Contents

Contents

Introduction

What do you do if your car has a water leak or if you discover oil on the ground beneath it? What if a warning light comes on? What could be the cause? Can I drive it? Do I need a breakdown service or a mechanic? How can I get it to a garage safely?

Our cars are essential to us, and it's hard to imagine being without them. If you drive one, then this is the book for you – even if you have minimal mechanical knowledge. You can avoid serious repair bills by learning exactly what to do when something goes wrong; doing the wrong thing could cost you a lot of money and be a real inconvenience. You can find out whether the car is safe to drive, and what action you need to take to complete a crucial journey or get your car to a garage.

Covering the most common problems that occur on modern vehicles, such as brake faults, oil and water leaks, starting issues, unusual noises/smells, and dashboard warning lights, this book is one of the most valuable items you can have in your car.

About the author & important information

About the author

For many years the author has been providing technical content for his automotive help website – carbasics.co.uk.

His engineering background, experience as a trainer, and passion for all things automotive have led to a skill for writing highly detailed yet easy-to-follow car DIY articles. Since 2006, carbasics.co.uk has helped thousands of car owners save money and keep their cars safe on the road. The success of his website and writing style have resulted in him being asked to write a number of automotive books.

Important information

If anything contained in this book contradicts what is written in the vehicle manufacturers' handbook, the advice in the official handbook should always take priority. The guidance in this book is general, so, whilst your car and its individual components may look a little different from the featured project cars and their components, the actions described will still be performed in essentially the same manner. All bolts, nuts and screws are turned anti-clockwise to undo, unless stated otherwise in the handbook. Always use the correct size tools (spanners, sockets, screwdrivers, etc) or you risk damaging parts of the car and increase the risk of injuring yourself.

one
Starting problems

1.1 Starter turns engine slowly but engine won't start

When turning the key to start the engine, the engine turns over slowly but won't start.

This indicates that the battery does not have enough charge. If you have access to a battery booster pack, or you can get someone to help jump-start the car, you should be able to get it started that way.

This problem can be caused by a number of things:
• A fault with the alternator, meaning that the battery is not getting recharged whilst you are driving.
• A faulty battery that is not holding its charge.
• A battery that is losing charge overnight, because something is drawing electricity from it.

These are the most common reasons a battery lacks charge, and the problem will need to be looked into

The car battery, the most common cause of car starting problems.

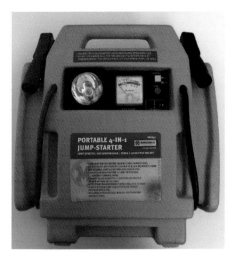

A typical battery booster can help to start a car with low battery level.

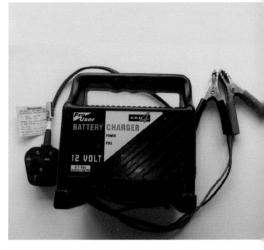

Use a battery charger to recharge a 'flat' battery. (Courtesy CarBasics.co.uk)

further to pinpoint the exact cause. You will need to get the car looked at by an auto-electrician to see which part needs replacing. If you have access to a voltmeter, connect it to the battery terminals and check the voltage output from the alternator. If the voltmeter reads around 13.8v or more, the alternator is good and will not need changing.

Less common faults that can give the same symptoms are a bad earth connection between engine and body, partially seized engine or seized clutch, amongst others.

Before buying a new battery, get the old one tested by a garage or car parts shop. They will have specialist equipment to test the battery fully, as its performance cannot be properly tested by using just a voltmeter. If both alternator and battery are in good condition, then something may be draining the battery when the car is not being used. You will need to take the car to an auto-electrician for diagnosis of the problem.

1.2 Starter turns engine strongly but engine won't start

This indicates that there is no fuel getting to the engine when you turn the key. You would get the same problem if you ran out of fuel, or if there was a fault with the ignition system, ie no spark at the sparkplugs to ignite the fuel (petrol engines). Diesel engines do not have sparkplugs, so for them you can rule this out and assume that non-starting is due to a fuelling issue.

The first thing to do is check that you have sufficient fuel. Check the fuel gauge on the dashboard, and think about when you last filled up. If you have run out of fuel, refer to chapter 16.1, 'Running out of fuel.'

If there is sufficient fuel in the tank, the fault may be that it's not getting to the engine freely. This can be caused by a blocked fuel filter, especially if the vehicle is getting old. Perhaps you recently ran very low on fuel, which may have drawn dirt from the bottom of the fuel tank into the system?

A faulty alternator can be the cause of a flat battery.

A typical alternator removed from car: it's being changed for a new unit.

Assessing whether the sparkplugs are working and fuel is getting to the engine can involve loosening injectors and checking sparkplugs – but this is really beyond first aid, as you'll need a workshop manual to help with procedure and diagnosis.

If you have car breakdown cover, it's time to call the organisation to see if it can get the car started and diagnose the problem.

1.3 No noise when ignition key turned

If the engine will not start when you turn the ignition, you first need to check whether the battery has power. Are any of the vehicle electrics working, such as dashboard lights, radio, headlights, etc? If headlights are working, but are very dim, then you have an almost-flat battery that will need to be recharged using a charger. You can also try using a battery booster pack, or getting someone to help jump start the car,

Also check to make sure that the battery terminals are securely tightened.

Caution! Don't allow the metal tool you use for this to short the positive terminal to an adjacent piece of metal. If you do manage to get the car started, you still need to establish the cause of the problem before it happens again.

If, when you turn the ignition key, there are no lights on the dashboard and no electrical items are working, you

Engine turns but won't fire, indicating a fuelling fault. Check for sufficient fuel.

Insufficient fuel getting to the fuel-injectors can prevent the engine from starting.

may have a totally flat battery that will need to be recharged and the cause looked into further.

If all of the electrics seem to be fine and you have sufficient power in the battery, the most likely cause is a faulty starter motor. This is what first rotates the engine to get it started. You may be able to check that all the wiring to the starter motor is still in place, as if this comes loose or has been damaged, it can prevent starter motor operation. If the wiring seems okay, you may need a new starter motor to get the car working again. However, the problem could also be a faulty alarm/immobiliser rather than starter motor. This will need to be looked at by a specialist.

Cars with faulty starter motors can often be got going by 'bump-starting' the car. This is the process of trying to start the car whilst it is rolling, either down a hill or whilst being pushed. Usually once rolling, you can depress the clutch pedal and put the vehicle into second gear, then with the ignition turned on (caution – make sure steering lock is off!) lift your foot off the clutch. This will engage the road wheels and turn the engine, basically replicating what the starter motor does when the car is stationary. Providing there is enough fuel and battery power, the car should start and drive okay. However, as soon as you turn off the ignition, you will not be able to start the car again without another bump-start. Please also note that you cannot bump-start vehicles that have automatic gearboxes. You may want to learn more about bump-starting cars before you attempt it yourself – the internet is a good place to start.

these issues. Check all of the wiring/ connections to the starter motor and solenoid in case they have come loose or have been damaged.

1.5 Car struggles to start from cold

There are quite a few reasons why a car might be difficult to start from cold, especially in the winter months. If your car is a diesel, make sure that you are letting the glow plugs warm sufficiently – read section 2.13 'Glow plug light (diesel engines)' for more information on this. Plenty of diesel drivers don't know they need to let the glow plugs operate for a few seconds before they start the engine.

If the weather is very cold and your car is not new, the problems you face could be caused by a number of things. Car batteries can be more prone to under-performing in cold weather, and alternators have to work harder, also providing power for lights, demisters, windscreen wipers, and heaters. Basically, the car's charging system has to work a lot harder in winter months, so ensure that everything is in full working order before an annoying difficult start becomes a full-blown breakdown.

Many garages will perform winter checks and will look at the health of the battery and alternator; this is well worth doing if you want to keep your car on the move. Also, for drivers of older diesel cars, in the winter months consider whether the glow plugs are performing as effectively as they used to, or some of them may no longer be working and need changing. (It's wise to change all of the glow plugs at the same time.)

Other problems could be to do with the ignition system on petrol/ gasoline-engined cars, particularly older vehicles. Moisture can get into the HT lead connections, sparkplugs

Nothing happens when ignition key is turned. Check for power to radio or dashboard lights.

1.4 Clicking noise but engine won't start

The clicking sound you can hear is the starter motor.

This noise signals that the starter motor is not turning over the engine. The most likely causes are a faulty starter motor, or a lack of battery power – see section 1.3 for addressing

A clicking noise and nothing else may indicate a faulty starter motor.

A typical starter motor with starter motor solenoid (arrowed) mounted on top.

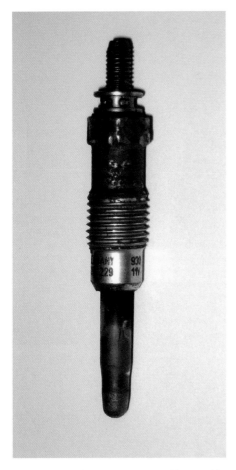

Failed glow plugs can cause problems with cold-starting on diesel engines.

1.6 Car struggles to start from hot

If your fuel-injected car struggles to start from hot, there is most likely a problem with an engine sensor. This is because the fuel is supplied under pressure and not generally routed near any heat sources, so should not be prone to evaporation problems.

Another point to consider with more modern fuel-injected engines (petrol or diesel) struggling to start from hot is the engine timing. If the engine timing, or any sensors related to engine timing, are faulty or incorrectly adjusted, the car may start fine from cold, but when hot (and especially in hot weather) may take a few seconds. If this is the case, take the vehicle for a diagnostic check and ask the technician to look at the engine timing.

Starter motors sticking in hot weather can be a problem: more so on older vehicles. This is something worth checking, as it can make engine starting difficult. A sticking starter or solenoid can be easily cleaned/replaced.

1.7 Engine starts, but stops straight away

If the engine starts but then stops straight away, you can normally dismiss any problems with the battery, alternator and starter motor, as it started to begin with. However, there are so many sensors on modern cars that it is impossible to point you directly to a specific cause.

Immediate stopping can often be caused by a fuelling problem. Ascertain whether there is a constant fuel supply to the fuel-injectors. Check for any blockages in fuel filters. Also, low fuel pressure caused by a faulty fuel pressure regulator or sensor can prevent the engine from starting. Locate the fuel pump, if possible (many are

could be getting old, and some vehicles also have an extra fuel-injector for cold starting that could be at fault. On modern vehicles, numerous sensors monitoring and controlling the starting of an engine could be at fault. Explain the problems to the mechanic and see what fault codes are returned from the diagnostic check. If your car is still under warranty, do not hesitate to take it back to your dealer and have it diagnose and rectify the fault.

immersed in the fuel tank), and check that you can hear it operating. You can also check that the relevant fuses are all operational.

In relation to petrol engines, establish that there is sufficient spark from the sparkplugs to ignite the fuel. Simple causes for a failed spark are a damaged or faulty plug, loose or faulty ignition leads, and on older cars a fault with the distributor.

The engine management light will most likely appear on your dashboard to indicate a fault. If any other lights are illuminated, you may need to refer to the vehicle owner's manual.

If you cannot establish why the engine will not keep running, find out what engine fault codes the ECU (Engine Control Unit – the computer that controls the engine) is producing. You can purchase your own engine fault code reader quite cheaply, and this

should pinpoint any faulty sensors that could be causing the problem. If you do not wish to do this yourself, and you are not a member of a rescue organisation, you will have to contact a garage to tow the car or send out a mobile mechanic with the relevant equipment.

If you have car breakdown cover, consider calling the policy provider and asking if they can identify and possibly repair the fault.

Also worth checking is the security immobiliser, if fitted. If this is not being turned off, or not operating correctly, it may stop the car from running. Have a look around the dashboard for any switches or LED lights, and check any paperwork that came with the car. If this is at fault then you may need to contact an alarm specialist or an auto-electrician to repair or bypass the faulty wiring.

two
Warning lights & gauges

This section covers what to do if certain warning lights come on at any point during your journey. As all cars vary in the type of warning lights they have, we will concentrate on only the most common and most important of them. If the vehicle has warning lights that are not included in this book, consult the car's user manual.

2.1 Engine warning light

This light normally illuminates when the ignition is turned on and goes out when the engine is started. If it stays on or comes on whilst driving, it is telling you that the car's ECU (Electronic Control Unit – its 'brain') has identified a fault that needs to be looked at.

There are so many sensors on modern cars that you will not be able to establish what the fault is without the car having a diagnostics check. Your local garage or dealership will need to connect your car to their computer and

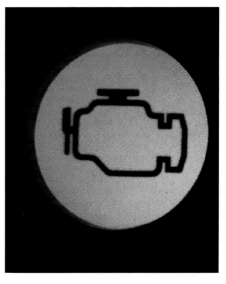

Typical engine fault warning light. Your car may need a diagnostics check.

extract the fault codes from the car's ECU.

These fault codes can help you, or your technician, diagnose the fault.

Can I still drive the car?

As long as you have the diagnostic check performed as soon as possible and there are no other faults with the car, it should be okay to drive. If you experience odd engine symptoms such as stalling, erratic idling or engine spluttering, you should only drive the car to the garage to avoid causing further damage.

Before starting or driving the vehicle, you MUST ensure that it has sufficient oil and water, and that there are no leaks.

2.2 Oil pressure warning light

This light normally illuminates when the ignition is turned on and goes out when the engine is started as oil pressure increases. Engines need good oil pressure in order to work correctly and not suffer serious damage.

If this light remains illuminated or illuminates whilst driving, pull over and turn off the engine as soon as possible. You will then need to check the engine oil level by inspecting the dipstick. If the oil level is low, topping-up to the necessary level may result in the warning light going out.

The car must not be driven if the oil pressure warning light stays on. DO NOT ignore it; it can be indicating a very serious problem with the engine ...

If the oil level is okay, the problem could possibly be a failed oil pressure switch/sensor, or worse, a failed oil pump or severely worn crankshaft bearings.

Listen for any unusual engine noises that could indicate a failed oil pump/ worn bearings. If there are none, it's likely that the oil pressure switch/sensor has failed and should be changed.

Typical oil pressure warning light. Check the engine oil level immediately.

Can I still drive the car?

Due to the possibility of an oil pump failure, it is not recommended that you drive the vehicle until the oil pressure fault has been thoroughly investigated. Start by changing the oil pressure switch, as this is the least expensive component. If you have it, call your car breakdown service to recover your car to a local garage.

There are a number of other indicators of oil pump problems, such as increased engine operating temperature, or increased engine noise, especially from the top of the engine. If the oil pump fails, it will cause serious and costly damage to the engine.

The need to top up engine oil occasionally to maintain the correct level is quite normal, particularly with the onset of dashboard 'oil level indicators.' Your vehicle user manual may advise how much oil the engine should be using. If you have to add oil to the engine quite frequently, something is wrong with it and needs to be looked at as soon as possible.

2.3 Alternator/battery warning light

This light normally illuminates when the ignition is turned on, and goes out when

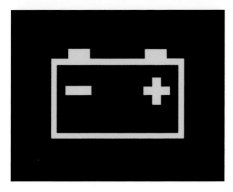

Typical alternator or battery warning light.
Check your charging system.

the engine is started. If this light comes on when you are driving, it is indicating that there is a fault with the charging system.

The first things that to look at are:
• Check that the battery terminals are securely in place (see section 8.1).
• Check whether the alternator drivebelt has broken or come off.
• Check that the alternator drivebelt is tight enough and is not slipping.

The alternator drivebelt should be in contact with the pulley at the end of the alternator. To check the drivebelt 'play,' hold it between your finger and thumb halfway between two pulleys and move it backwards and forwards. It should feel quite tight and only move about 1in. If the play is more than this, consider having the alternator tension adjusted or the belt replaced.

If both of these are okay, assume that either the battery or the alternator needs to be replaced. If you do not know how to check which of these needs to be replaced, have the car looked at by an auto-electrician.

Can I still drive the car?
If the alternator belt is no longer in place, you should not drive the car,

as it is possible the belt is also driving the coolant pump. If coolant is not pumped around the engine, it will overheat and this can cause very costly damage.

If the alternator drivebelt is in place and not loose, you should be okay to complete your journey, providing it is not a long haul. However, understand that if the fault is with the charging system, such as the alternator, the battery will not be recharging as you are driving. Low battery voltage on modern cars can cause lots of problems, and if you are driving a petrol/gasoline-engined car, eventually there will be no more power to the sparkplugs and the engine will stop running.

Battery warning light tips
If you have identified that the fault lies with the alternator and it is not charging the battery, turn off as many electrical components as possible, eg interior heater, radio, air-conditioning etc. This will ensure that the power remaining in the battery is only being used for essentials, which may help you reach your destination.

It takes less battery power to keep a car running than to restart it. So if you have a battery warning light fault and a journey to complete, be careful not to stall the car, as there may not be enough battery power to start it again.

2.4 ABS warning light

If the ABS light has come on, first make sure that it actually is the ABS light and not the warning light for the whole braking system. You may need to refer to the car's user manual to check if the illuminated light is multifunction, which could indicate either problem.

For the purposes of this section, it is assumed that the light is not multifunctional and the car does have

Example of ABS warning light.

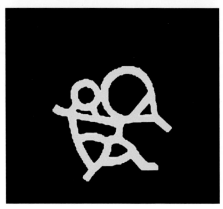

Example of airbag warning light.

an ABS fault. For braking system faults, see chapter 2.9, 'Brake fluid level warning light.'

If it is definitely the ABS that's faulty, the first thing to do is turn the ignition off and on again to see if this fixes the problem. There may be a fault with the ABS module/sensor, or perhaps a broken wire or loose connector. Gget your car diagnosed by a technician using the relevant fault code reader. There is usually a small cost for this, but the code retrieved from the car should help identify the fault.

Can I still drive my car?
Yes, but you must be aware that without the ABS working, your car's stopping distances will be increased, reducing your safety. Have your car's ABS system inspected and repaired as soon as possible.

2.5 Airbag warning light

With most cars, when you turn on the ignition the airbag light should come on for a short while and then go out. If the warning light stays on all the time, this indicates a fault within the airbag operating system.

Can I still drive the car?
The car is still driveable, but in the event of an accident, a fault in the airbag system may result in the airbags not being deployed. It is, therefore, essential to get the fault inspected by a garage as soon as possible.

2.6 Temperature gauge stopped working

If the temperature gauge seems to have stopped working, ie is showing no temperature at all, stop the car immediately and turn off the engine.

A temperature gauge that was working and then seems to stop working can be an indication of a loss of engine coolant. Visually check the coolant level in the transparent expansion tank in the engine bay. It should be between 'max' and 'min.'

If the level is okay and there are no apparent leaks, it's likely that the sensor that sends the signal to the temperature gauge has failed or become disconnected. If your car has lost engine coolant or has a coolant leak,

If your car's engine temperature gauge stops showing a reading, turn off the engine and check the coolant level immediately.

refer to chapter 15 'Engine coolant' for further advice.

Can I still drive the car?

If you have sufficient coolant in the engine cooling system and it just appears that a sensor has failed, it should be okay to drive the car. Get this fault investigated as soon as possible, because engine coolant temperature is critically important to the car's well-being.

2.7 Temperature gauge showing very hot

If the indicated temperature is very high for the weather or driving conditions, turn off the vehicle as soon as possible. A low coolant level is one of the most common causes of an overheating engine. Check that there is enough coolant in the expansion tank: ie between the 'min' and 'max' marks. Top up if necessary.

Caution! Wait until the engine has cooled before removing the expansion chamber cap.

Radiator fan

The radiator fan should start operating at a certain temperature, helping to reduce the heat of the engine coolant.

Typical temperature warning light. Check engine coolant levels immediately if this comes on.

When the engine is hot, you should be able to hear the radiator fan operating. The radiator fan will be located directly behind the radiator at the front of the engine bay, between the headlights. If it does not appear to be working, the engine can overheat. Check the radiator fan fuse and all of the wiring/plugs to ensure it is working correctly. Normally, the engine coolant thermostat controls the fan. If this has failed then the fan will not operate.

Can I still drive the car?

If you do need to complete your journey, you must make sure you have plenty of coolant in the cooling system, and make regular stops to let the engine cool down.

Letting the engine overheat, or run out of coolant, can cause catastrophic damage to the engine. If you have lost engine coolant, or have a coolant leak, then refer to chapter 15, 'Engine coolant' for further advice.

Hot engine tips

• If an overheating engine is being caused by hot weather and sitting in traffic, turn on the car cabin heater to full/hot for a while. This may help reduce the temperature or stop it increasing, as it will draw some of the heat out of the engine cooling system.

• Drive with the air-conditioning turned off. Air-conditioning puts a load on the engine, meaning that it will have to work harder, and hence be hotter.
• If you've had to top up the engine coolant level, check in the engine bay for signs of a leak. Check all the hoses, the radiator and under the car: see chapter 15.2, 'There is coolant leaking.'
• Make regular stops on your journey, opening the bonnet to let the engine cool down.
• Don't drive in the rush hour, as sitting in slow traffic will make the car overheat. Wait for the traffic to die down, and whilst you are waiting the engine will be cooling.

2.8 Electronic power steering warning light

If your car has electronic power steering (EPS) there will be a motor, for assisting the steering, attached to the steering column or steering rack. This kind of system removes the requirement for the traditional hydraulic system, and is becoming much more common.

If your EPS warning light comes on, you may be experiencing an intermittent or full loss of power steering, resulting in the steering becoming heavy. You will need to take your car to your local garage to have a diagnostic check performed on the vehicle. Your local garage or dealership will need to extract the fault codes from your car's computer. Common EPS faults occur with the electronic torque sensor and the electronic control unit. If your car is still under warranty, any fault finding and subsequent repair charges should be covered by your car dealership.

If your car has a 'city mode' – a mode used for parking or town driving in which the steering is made very light

– try turning this off to see if it helps. Also, try turning off the engine for a few minutes and then restarting, which may also solve the problem. Be aware that if either of these methods do rectify the fault, it will only be a temporary fix and the problem will return. You should still take your car to your local garage as soon as possible to get the fault diagnosed.

Can I still drive the car?

Yes, you should still be able to drive the car as your steering wheel is still linked directly to the wheels, only now there will be no power assistance when steering. You will find that the steering becomes heavier, especially at slow speeds and whilst parking.

Warning! If the car's EPS warning light has come on, but your power steering still feels as though it is working fine, be aware that it could stop working at any moment, and, although your car will still be driveable, the steering could suddenly become heavy. Proceed with caution, and remain alert about the possible change in the steering.

Tip If your EPS does have a 'city' or 'parking' mode to make the steering lighter whilst town driving in traffic or when parking, make sure you turn it off when you don't need it. These settings make the steering motor work harder, and using them continuously can cause problems. Refer to your vehicle handbook for 'best practice' regarding using your EPS.

Tip If you keep getting an intermittent power steering fault, make sure that the battery and charging system are working fully. Ensure that there are no loose connections at the battery and that it is fully charged.

Typical brake warning light. Check brake fluid level immediately.

2.9 Brake warning light

With the ignition on, your brake warning light should remain on whilst the handbrake is engaged and go out when it is released.

Low brake fluid level

The most common cause for the brake warning light coming on is that the brake fluid needs to be topped up.

You will need to top up the brake fluid level via the reservoir in the engine bay. Look in your car's user manual for the correct type of brake fluid, which can be purchased from your local car parts shop.

When topping-up your brake fluid, take care not to spill any – it is corrosive and can damage paintwork and other car parts. Try not to get any on your hands, and clean small spills with a wet cloth.

Worn brake pads

On many cars this light also informs the driver that the brake pads are worn and need replacement.

Handbrake switch

A reason for the brake warning light not going out when the handbrake is released is that the handbrake switch is faulty or needs adjusting.

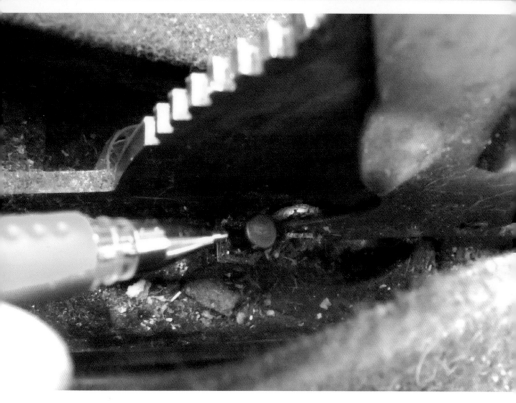

Check that the handbrake switch is not faulty or in need of adjustment.

Can I still drive the car?

Unless you have confirmed that there is sufficient brake fluid in the system and the fault lies elsewhere (ie with the handbrake switch), it is not recommended you drive the car. Call your breakdown service and get the car recovered to a garage.

Tip If your brake warning light never comes on, it is likely that the dashboard bulb behind the light has failed and needs to be changed.

2.10 Tyre pressure monitoring system warning light

If fitted, this normally illuminates when the ignition is turned on and goes out when the engine is started. There are air pressure sensors for each wheel, which will trigger the TPMS warning light to alert the driver to a problem.

The TPMS warning light indicates an unsafe change in the air pressure in one of your tyres. Usually a 25 per cent drop in pressure will trigger the warning light in the dashboard.

Usually, the light staying on means a tyre pressure fault, but if the TPMS light flashes on and off, this indicates a fault with the TPMS system, not a tyre pressure fault. Refer to your car's user manual for further advice regarding the correct operation of the system fitted to your car.

Typical TPMS warning light.

If all tyre pressures are correct, but the TPMS warning light is still activated, this indicates that there is a problem with the system that needs investigating by your garage. They will perform a diagnostic check on the car and identify what fault codes are being presented. The fault codes should identify which of the system's components are at fault.

Can I still drive the car?
Driving a car with low tyre pressures can be dangerous. A faulty TPMS system will give you no indication of a problem with your tyres. The car can still be driven, but you will have to make regular checks on your car's tyres until the system is repaired.

2.11 Seatbelt warning light

Check your car's user manual for the correct operation of your seatbelt warnings, as some vehicles will only warn you for a short period or will only work for the driver's seat. Some systems will only warn you of an unfastened seatbelt over a certain speed. There will be a warning light on the dashboard, and on some vehicles this is also accompanied by a buzzer. The system will establish that someone is sitting in the seat, and whether or not they have fastened their seatbelt. This is done by use of a sensor in the seat to detect driver or passenger weight, and also a sensor in the seatbelt

Typical seatbelt warning light, sometimes accompanied by a buzzer.

buckle to detect that the belt has been fastened.

Other than taking your car for a diagnostics check, the only check you can really perform on your seatbelt warning system is ensuring the wiring/ plugs to the seat and seatbelt sensors are still firmly in place. If you do rectify faulty wiring or a loose plug, you may need to have the seatbelt system reset to clear the warning light.

A diagnostics check on the vehicle will reveal a fault code identifying the precise problem.

Can I still drive the car?
Yes you can, but be aware that if it is fitted with other safety devices, such as seatbelt pre-tensioners or side airbags, they may not operate correctly.

2.12 Diesel particulate filter (DPF) warning light

DPF warning lights, also referred to as the DPF/CAT light, are fitted to many diesel-engined vehicles from around 2009 onwards. Particulate filters are designed to capture soot from the exhaust to reduce emissions.

The DPF warning light will come on at a preset point (for example, when the filter is 45 per cent full). Refer to your car's user manual for information on how it should operate, and what you can do to turn it off again.

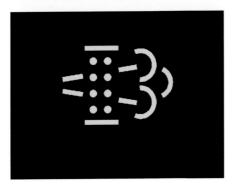

Typical diesel particulate filter warning light.

It may be your driving style that is causing your car's DPF to fill up with soot, as it is a high exhaust gas temperature that facilitates the automatic cleaning of the filter (referred to as regeneration). Regeneration is normally controlled via the ECU, which alters the car's fuelling and timing to increase exhaust temperature until the captured soot is burnt off. However, with town/stop-start driving, the active regeneration process may not complete its cycle, and the filter will fill up.

Take your car for a prolonged fast drive, say 10-20 minutes at speeds greater than 40mph, or better still, motorway speed. This should increase the temperature in the exhaust, and the DPF will perform its regeneration. You should then find that the warning light goes off.

Although your car is still driveable with the DPF warning light on, ignoring it for any length of time will result in having to replace the DPF completely ... and they are not cheap.

If you have driven the car as suggested and the light does not go off, take the vehicle to a garage for an inspection.

Tip An intermittent DPF warning light (one that comes on and goes off) is telling you that the filter is starting to fill up and you need to adjust your driving for a short period (confirm this in the user manual). Eventually, the warning light will come on permanently, requiring attention.

2.13 Glow plug light (diesel engines)

When the engine is cold and you turn on the ignition, this light should illuminate for a short period. If the light does not come on, it means that there is a fault with the glow plug system.

The purpose of the glow plug is to pre-heat the engine before starting. Without pre-heating, diesel engines are difficult – if not impossible – to start, because the diesel fuel will be too cold to ignite.

Glow plug changing
Changing your car's glow plugs should rectify the problem. It is recommended that you change all of the glow plugs at the same time. There should be one per cylinder (typically four in total).

Glow plug timer relay
It is worth checking that the timer relay controlling the glow plugs is working. You may be able to identify its location via your car user manual, or by searching online.

Can I still drive the car?
Yes, once the engine is started the glow

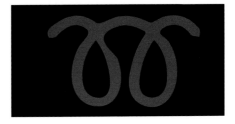

Typical glow plug light.

plugs no longer operate. However, you will experience difficulty starting the car, especially during cold weather.

Glow plug tips

• Starting the engine whilst the glow plug is in its heating cycle (warning light on) will overheat and damage the glow plugs, thus shortening their life. Put another way, don't start the engine until the glow plug light has gone out.
• Do not buy cheap glow plugs, as they will not last. Buy exactly the right glow plug for your vehicle, and ensure they are from a reputable manufacturer.
• Ensure that your car's charging system (battery, alternator, etc) are in good order, as the operation of glow plugs can be affected by low voltages during charging.

2.14 Fuel filter water trap (diesel engines)

This light should briefly illuminate when the ignition is turned on. If it does not go out, this normally indicates that there is excess water in the vehicle's fuel filter water trap, or that the fuel filter needs to be changed.

On certain vehicles, you can perform a drain to remove the excess water that the filter trap has captured. If you are able to perform this procedure yourself, it should be outlined in your vehicle user manual. Alternatively you will need to take the car to your local garage.

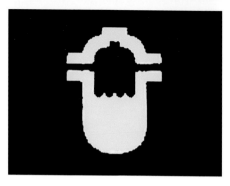

Typical fuel filter water trap warning light.

On some vehicles, it may not be possible to just drain off the excess water, and you will need to have the fuel filter replaced.

Can I still drive the car?

Normally the vehicle will be okay to drive. The warning should be designed to notify you that it needs attention, not that the vehicle is undriveable. If you do not perform the draining procedure or do not change the fuel filter as soon as possible, the excess water will start to cause other problems with the vehicle.

Tip If you have just filled the car with fuel and subsequently the warning light comes on, consider the possibility that the new fuel is contaminated. In this situation, stop the car and get the matter investigated further. It may be a good idea to contact your breakdown service provider for further advice.

three
Noises

You will get to know the sound of your car as you live with it and drive it. How your car sounds should be the same every day, and changes may be an indication that something is different. Noises are a good way of identifying problems, and this section covers the most common ones and their possible causes.

3.1 Engine bay noises

The engine sounds extremely loud
If the engine suddenly gets extremely loud just after starting or whilst driving, turn it off immediately. This is an indication that something serious has gone wrong, and driving any further will cause major problems. If the timing belt has failed or has changed position, the internal parts of the engine can come into contact with each other and cause catastrophic damage.

Timing belts should be changed at regular intervals, as recommended by

Really loud engine noise can indicate a timing problem. Turn off the engine immediately.

the manufacturer. This is one area of car maintenance that you should not cut corners on, because the cost for neglecting the car's timing belt can be extremely high.

If you are at all concerned that the timing belt may have failed or moved, do not drive the car. Arrange to have it inspected where it is, or get it towed to a garage.

Can I still drive the car?
No, do not start the engine. Have it checked out immediately by a mechanic. Call your breakdown service to have the car towed to a garage and investigated.

Loose engine covers
Anything that sounds like a slight rattle or vibration may well be one of the many engine covers, partitions or the engine undertray. If the car generally drives smoothly, and without any loss in power, it is likely that something has worked loose, and is nothing major.

With the engine running, listen to where the sound seems to be coming from.

Caution! If you do this with the bonnet/hood open, do not allow loose clothing to dangle into the compartment and do not put your hands in there. With the engine off, check the plastic covers and partitions for security and that all the fixings are in place. Anything that is loose and flapping around is likely to vibrate when you are driving along.

Can I still drive the car?
If the vibrating noise tends to go away as you steadily rev the engine, you're probably fine to proceed with your journey. However, check the engine bay to make sure nothing is about to drop off and cause damage to any other parts.

Failed engine mount
This is generally aimed at older or high-powered vehicles, as most modern vehicle engine mounts should not fail.

Check around the engine bay for loose engine covers that could be vibrating.

Look at the engine whilst it is running. If it seems to be moving around and vibrating a lot more than usual it is highly likely that an engine mounting has failed.

Can I still drive the car?
Yes, you can still drive the car for a short distance, but you must get the mount replaced or repaired as soon as possible. Driving with a broken engine mount will put stress on other car components, such as the other engine mounts, as well as driveshafts, gearbox linkages, and anything else connected to the engine.

Squealing sound when accelerating
This is most probably the sound of a drivebelt slipping. You may get this sound more when first starting the car, with it beginning to disappear as the car warms up. Cars can have many

drivebelts, and they all need to be in good order for the car to work correctly. Sometimes the squealing noise will go away, but finding out which belt is causing the problem should be a priority.

The most likely causes of a squealing noise when accelerating are a slipping alternator drivebelt or a slipping power steering drivebelt. It is more likely that a faulty power steering belt will squeal when you are turning the steering wheel at low speeds, thus putting the pump under more load, while the alternator drivebelt is most likely to squeal on initial start-up.

It is likely that the drivebelt tensioner needs to be adjusted or replaced as soon as possible before the loose belt comes off, or snaps.

A seized power steering pump or water pump can cause the same type of noise, but you will probably also be

Check that timing belt covers are securely clipped in place. (Courtesy CarBasics.co.uk)

Check the tension of your car's alternator drivebelt, as it may be loose and slipping.

Squealing when accelerating can be caused by a slipping alternator belt.

able to hear a groaning noise from those parts when the engine is idling.

Can I still drive the car?

If the squealing is constant and it is a power steering pump, water pump or similar that has failed or seized, then you should not drive the car and it should be repaired as soon as possible.

If the squealing is constant and from a belt, then it should also be looked at as soon as possible. This is because the belt that's slipping could be driving an important component, such as the alternator, power steering or water pump inefficiently.

If the belt squealing is intermittent and mainly occurs when the car is first started and then goes away quite quickly, the car should still be okay to drive for a short while. However, the fault will still need to be attended to, as it will only get worse over time.

Hissing noise/steam coming from under bonnet

If there is a hissing sound coming from under the bonnet, the most likely cause is a fault with the engine cooling system. That sound is probably steam escaping from a leaking hose or radiator.

The first thing to do is stop the car and turn off the engine. Then check the coolant level by observing the transparent expansion tank – the coolant level should be between the 'min' and 'max' markings. It is important to turn the engine off as soon as possible; you do not want to run it without any coolant.

Caution! Removing the expansion tank cap on a hot or overheating engine can put you at risk of scalding from escaping steam. Consider putting a cloth over it to protect yourself before

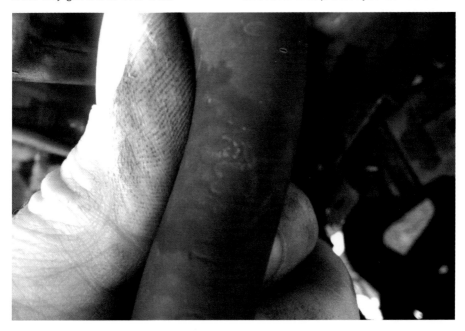

Inspect hoses for splits and holes. (Courtesy CarBasics.co.uk)

Check security of water hoses from beneath the car as well as from above.

you unscrew it, or better still, let the engine cool down first.

Top up the coolant level if necessary and then restart the engine.

Caution! Do not allow loose clothing to dangle into the engine compartment and do not put your hands in there.

Check the engine bay to find out where the hissing is coming from. Look for steam and also water coming from any hoses or the radiator. Also, check on the ground under the engine to see if there is anything dripping.

Can I still drive the car?
If you have identified a relatively minor coolant leak but need to complete your journey, it is essential that you keep the coolant topped-up. If the engine overheats due to a lack of coolant, the damage to it could be catastrophic.

If you have a major leak, do not drive the vehicle. You will need to get the part replaced and the coolant system refilled. Contact your breakdown service and have the vehicle recovered to a nearby garage.

3.2 Exhaust noises

The exhaust is much noisier than normal
If everything else with the car seems okay, but the noise from the exhaust is noticeably louder, the chances are that you have a leak in the exhaust system.

With the engine running, stand outside the car and listen for exhaust gases escaping from anywhere other than the tailpipe. You may also be able to smell the exhaust gases coming from underneath the car, which may help you to identify the leak.

You may also be able to see where the exhaust leak is, as there may be

Check for exhaust leaks by looking for soot build-up. (Courtesy CarBasics.co.uk)

The exhaust should be suspended beneath the car via rubber hangers. Ensure these are secure.

a soot build up around the damaged area.

Caution! Do not touch the exhaust until it has cooled sufficiently.

Can I still drive the car?
Yes, small exhaust leaks should not cause any noticeable difference to the performance and feel of the vehicle. It may be a little louder and the fuel consumption may increase a little. However, it is important to repair or replace the faulty exhaust component as soon as possible, as the problem will only get worse. You can purchase repair products for small exhaust leaks such as 'exhaust repair bandage' and exhaust putty – see chapter 6.3, 'Exhaust is leaking.'

Banging from exhaust
If the exhaust is hitting the underside of the car or a part of the vehicle chassis you will hear it as you drive along. It will sound like someone is trying to get in through the car floor. If this is happening, a part of the exhaust or an exhaust mounting has failed. Either take the car to an exhaust specialist to

identify and repair the problem, or take a look at it yourself.

Caution! If you are going to perform any work underneath your car, make sure that you work safely using the correct jack, axle stands and wheel chocks. Refer to the user manual for the correct jacking points. Never work under a car on the jack alone.

Can I still drive the car?
You can still drive the car, but be aware that the problem will not go away if you ignore it. It will get worse and eventually this will result in a part of the exhaust failing and needing repair.
Equipment like catalytic converters, diesel particulate filters and exhaust sensors will not like being banged about and any delay in repairing the exhaust can cause damage to these components.

3.3 Wheel noises

Humming/vibrating from wheels at higher speeds
If your car makes a humming or grumbling noise that seems to increase

Checking the tension of the power steering belt. Too much movement may mean a new belt is required.

or decrease with vehicle speed, the most likely cause is a faulty wheel bearing, assuming that all other components on the car are working satisfactorily and there are no problems with the brakes.

The most common wheel bearings to fail are those on the front of the vehicle, as they carry the most load when driving.

You may also notice that the noise becomes louder when turning in one direction. For example, a vehicle with a faulty wheel bearing on the left may get quieter as you turn right, as you are lessening the load on the faulty bearing. Conversely, it may get louder as you turn left.

Changing a wheel bearing does require a good level of mechanical skill and a good set of mechanic's tools. Consider getting the fault investigated further by your local garage, and have it perform the repair. Also, if you are not 100 per cent sure that it is a faulty wheel bearing, you should get another opinion.

Tip As you are driving along and the noise starts, take your foot off the accelerator pedal and depress the clutch to quieten the engine. This may help you to identify which side the noise is coming from. Having the windows open may also help.

Tip After driving the car, carefully feel the wheel centres to see if any of them seem to be hotter than the others.

Caution! Take care not to touch the brake discs or pads, as they may be hot.

Can I still drive the car?
If you have established that a wheel bearing needs changing, be aware that the fault will only worsen with every wheel rotation. You will most likely have a damaged bearing with broken parts in it and no lubrication.

Caution! Driving the car will put you at risk of the wheel bearing failing completely and causing damage to other parts of the car.

Squealing noise when turning steering wheel

If you experience a high pitched squealing or screeching noise when turning the steering wheel, there is a fault with the power steering system. If you have a faulty power steering drivebelt or pump, the noise will most often occur when the vehicle is stationary, at slow speeds, or on full-lock.

You should not experience this type of noise if the vehicle is fitted with electronic power steering (EPS).

Most commonly, this noise will be coming from the power steering drivebelt slipping when it is under load. The most common cause of a power steering belt slipping is age – they will stretch over time. Although the vehicle may allow for some adjustment of the drivebelt tension, it is advised that you get the drivebelt changed as soon as possible.

Another possible cause for this noise may be that the power steering system is low on fluid, or that the

pump itself is faulty. First check the power steering fluid level and top up if necessary. If you do not have much mechanical experience, you may want to have this performed by your local garage, as the procedure is not often covered in the car user manual.

Can I still drive the car?

The car can still be driven, but if the drivebelt comes off or snaps, you must be aware that you will be left without any power steering, and if this happens whilst you are driving it could result in an accident.

If the cause of the noise is low power steering fluid level, driving the vehicle could cause damage to the power steering pump, resulting in it needing to be replaced.

The fault will continue to get worse until the necessary parts have been repaired or changed, and you must be aware of the potential for abrupt changes in steering feel whilst driving.

Tip If the power steering fluid needs

If you hear knocking when braking, check that the wheel nuts/bolts are tight.

Remove the wheel and check the security of the brake components.

Inspecting brakes: ensure that brake pad retaining springs are securely in place.

to be topped up, ascertain why, as there may be a leak.

3.4 Brake noises

Knocking noise when braking (front)
This can be a difficult area in which to identify the specific problem, because there are quite a few things that could be causing the noise. Also, the older the car gets, the more parts will wear out and the more possible causes there will be. The most likely cause will be a worn or broken suspension part, and this section offers guidance to help you identify the problem.

If the vehicle is fitted with ABS (anti-lock braking system) we will assume that the knocking occurs under normal braking. If it is only occurring under very heavy braking, it is likely that the ABS is causing it, which is totally normal. You may also feel the knocking through the brake pedal when the ABS is active.

The first thing to check is that the wheel nuts/bolts are all secured tightly. It sounds obvious, but this is a simple process and should be the first thing to be ruled out. If any of the bolts require tightening, be sure to check all the others too.

Secondly, check that the brake pads are secured in place, without any movement, and that any securing/vibration springs/clips are in place.

With the wheel now off and the brake components inspected, have a look at the suspension components for signs of a break, excessive movement, or any contact points (see tips).

Here are some of the most common suspension problems that should be inspected:
• Broken suspension spring.
• Worn anti-roll bar bushes.
• Worn or broken drop links.
• Worn trackrod end wear.
• Worn lower ball joint.

Make sure the suspension springs are secure and not broken.

If the car has any other symptoms, such as pulling to one side, refer to the relevant section in this book for advice.

Refer to chapter 14, 'Suspension/wheels/tyres,' for further advice.

Can I still drive the car?
In most instances, yes, it should be okay to drive the car. However, be aware that the fault is very likely to affect handling, so you should drive accordingly and have the faulty part identified and replaced quickly.

Tip If the vehicle is under warranty, take it back and let the garage have the fun of trying to trace what's causing the knocking noise.

Tip Checking for contact points on suspension parts may help you identify the cause of the problem – these parts should not come into contact with each other. If there are any small surface areas on the suspension parts that appear to have been rubbed clean or are shiny, then this indicates that there has been contact and that the parts are worn, broken or maladjusted.

Knocking noise when braking (rear)
The most likely cause will be a worn or broken suspension part, but you should also inspect the rear brakes to ensure that everything is firmly in place. Check that all of the wheel nuts/bolts are tight. There are fewer suspension parts to wear out on the rear of the car, so, compared with the front suspension, it may be easier to diagnose the fault.

Check that the rear suspension springs are not broken or unseated.

If the car is fitted with rear drop links (many BMWs, for example), check these are okay and there is no wear in the bushes.

Check that the rear shock absorber is securely in place and not leaking.

If you cannot identify the cause of the knocking, you will need to have a mechanic look into the problem.

Can I still drive the car?
In most instances, yes, it should be okay to drive the car. However, be aware that the fault is very likely to affect handling, so drive accordingly and have the faulty part identified and replaced promptly.

Grinding/scraping noise when braking
The most common cause of a grinding noise under braking is that the brake

pads on the car are worn down to their metal backings and need replacing.

Another cause could be debris between the brake pad and disc, or stuck in the calliper and rubbing on the disc. Take off the wheels and inspect the disc surface for uneven wear.

Can I still drive the car?
Caution! Worn brake pads will seriously limit the car's braking ability, and must be changed as soon as possible. If you discover your pads are worn to the metal, you shouldn't drive the car.

Delaying changing the brake pads may cause damage to the brake discs. They could overheat and warp, or they could begin to wear out more quickly or unevenly. This could result in needing to have the brake discs changed too, instead of just the pads.

Squealing when braking
This does not necessarily indicate a braking system fault. If you have recently had the brake pads or discs changed, and are experiencing squealing under braking, there is probably no problem and the noise will likely stop over time. The squealing noise is caused by a change in the frequency at which the brake and disc friction materials rub together. As the friction materials wear away (under normal braking) the squealing sound will probably disappear.

Can I still drive the car?
Yes, providing that the braking performance of the car has not been affected it should be safe to drive the car, and the noise should go away on its own as the brake pads wear.

3.5 Suspension noises

Knocking noise from the front on bumpy ground
The most likely cause of this type of

Knocking from the front over bumpy ground can be caused by worn drop links.

noise is worn anti-roll bar drop links. These are the bars that connect the anti-roll bar to the suspension arm. When the bushes inside them wear out they will make a banging sound, especially when you are travelling over speed bumps. These are relatively easy to change, and should be available from your local car parts shop.

Can I still drive the car?
Yes, but get the parts changed as soon as possible, as if they fail it could result in other damage occurring to the vehicle.

3.6 Clutch noises

Noise when depressing the clutch pedal
If you experience a grating or grumbling noise when depressing the clutch pedal,

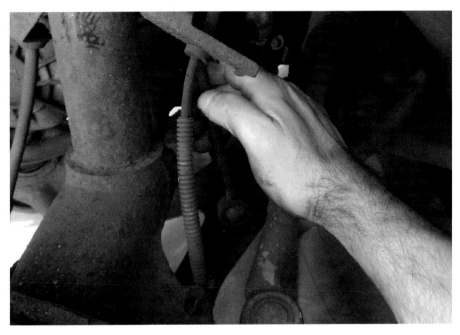

Checking drop links for signs of movement and wear. (Courtesy CarBasics.co.uk)

Investigate any noise you hear when the clutch lever is depressed.

this is likely to be caused by a worn thrust bearing (also called a throw out bearing) within the clutch.

Can I still drive the car?
Yes, but this bearing will probably fail at some point and you should get it changed before this happens. Whilst the mechanic is replacing the thrust bearing, it would be a good idea to change the other wearing parts in the clutch, like the friction plate and cover,

especially if the car has done a lot of miles.

Changing a clutch can be quite a labour intensive job, so whilst the mechanic has the car stripped down to replace the thrust bearing, it does make sense to have the complete clutch replaced.

3.7 Under-car noises

Knocks or bangs seeming to come from

Knocking from beneath the car could be due to a loose exhaust system. (Courtesy CarBasics.co.uk)

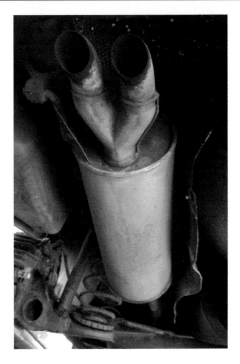

underneath the car when driving are most likely coming from the exhaust system.

Check that the exhaust is mounted securely in place and is not banging on the underside of the car. Have a look under there and give it a shake (when cold!). If it seems very loose, there may be a faulty hanging bracket or missing exhaust rubber hanger.

Can I still drive the car?
Typically, yes, providing that the exhaust is not going to drop off and cause further damage to your car or cause an accident. If you are in any doubt, you should not drive the car, and should contact your breakdown service or local garage.

As soon as possible, get the faulty part repaired or replaced.

four
Smells

Unusual smells are always worth investigating, as they may indicate that something needs to be repaired or replaced.

4.1 Sweet smell

A sweet smell in the car (like maple syrup or butterscotch) is most likely the result of an engine coolant leak. Anti-freeze (or engine coolant) smells very sweet when it has been heated by the engine, and the smell is most likely coming from a leaking hose, the radiator, or the heating system.

Stop the car and look for any leaks in the engine bay. First check the level in the expansion tank to see if any coolant has been lost. If the level is okay, start the car and look in the engine bay to see if you can find the leak. Check the coolant hoses and radiator, and have a look under the car to see if there is anything dripping.

If you find a leaking hose or a radiator leak, you will need to fix it by either changing the part or using a 'stop-leak treatment' (for radiators) or 'hose repair' for coolant hoses.

If you cannot find a leak in the engine bay, check whether the leak is coming from the heating system inside the car. Check the carpets in the driver and passenger side footwell for dampness. Also, with the engine running, if the smell only occurs when the heater is blowing hot, it could be the heater matrix or relevant pipework that is leaking. You may be able to fix this leak by using a 'stop-leak' treatment.

Can I still drive the car?
If the vehicle has plenty of coolant in the engine cooling system, and the leak is small, the car should be okay to drive. Be aware that any small leak has the potential to become a big leak very fast, causing the loss of coolant and overheating the engine.

A sweet smell coming from the car is usually caused by anti-freeze, so look for a coolant leak.

Coolant/anti-freeze leak indicated here by white furry deposit.

Tip Always make sure you keep a large bottle of water in the car in case you need to top the engine cooling system up.

4.2 Fishy smell

Burning rubber or melting plastic will give off a fishy smell. If you experience this smell coming from your car, look into it straight away. It usually indicates that some parts are rubbing together that should not be, or that a plastic part is melting or touching something hot. You will need to have a look around the engine bay for the cause of the smell.

Look for such things as a plastic engine cover rubbing on a moving part, or a piece of wiring or rubber hose touching a hot exhaust and melting.

Caution! Beware of moving parts in the engine bay, and catching loose clothing, jewellery and long hair. Consider investigating the smell with the engine turned off.

Check that all of the engine drivebelts are in place and running correctly, ie alternator drivebelt or air-con pump drivebelt. A faulty component could cause belt slip, creating the smell. Make sure that none of the plastic belt covers are loose and touching the moving parts.

Check the tyres are not catching on any bodywork, and that there is no debris trapped under the wheel arches.

Also check under the car in case something, like a plastic bag, has melted onto the hot exhaust.

Can I still drive the car?

This depends on the cause of the smell – it could be extremely serious if not dealt with immediately. For example, if the car has wiring melting onto a hot

Fishy smells can be caused by burning plastic. Check there are no loose engine covers in contact with hot or moving components.

exhaust, it is not recommended to drive the car, but if you have a drivebelt cover that is slightly rubbing then it would be okay to drive until the problem is fixed.

4.3 Smells like burning paper

If you are getting a smell like burning newspaper, the most likely cause is a slipping clutch.

Usually it is friction material that is causing the smell. A slipping friction plate causes the friction material on both its faces to overheat. You may

An old clutch exposed: a burning paper smell may signal a slipping clutch friction plate.

experience the smell more if you have been driving fast and performing fast gear changes, or if you have been towing a caravan or trailer and the clutch is slipping as you pull away. Also if you 'hold' the car stationary on a gradient by slipping the clutch instead of using the handbrake (bad practice!).

If you experience this smell, refer to the index to identify other problems that would indicate a slipping clutch.

Can I still drive the car?
Yes. However, if the clutch is slipping and you choose to do nothing then eventually it will fail completely and the car will be undriveable.

Have a look at chapter 11, which gives advice on how to drive with a slipping clutch.

4.4 Burning oil smell

Most commonly this will occur if engine oil has come into contact with a very hot part of the car, such as an exhaust.

If you have recently had the oil changed or topped-up, it's possible that there may be an oil spill that should burn off quite quickly, making the smell go away.

With regard to oil leaks, you will need to identify where the leak is coming from and how severe it is. Check that there is sufficient oil in the engine, in case the leak has been happening for some time.

Also check the ground where the car is most often parked to see if there has been any oil dripping. This might give you an indication of how long it has

Oil coming from the rocker/cam cover is a common leak.

Oil leaking onto a hot exhaust manifold can cause a strong burning smell.

After discovering an oil leak, make regular checks on the engine oil level.

been leaking or how big the leak may be.

Can I still drive the car?
Providing that there is sufficient oil in the engine and the oil leak is only small, the car is okay to drive until the repair has been made. Make sure you clean off as much excess oil as possible from in and around the leak, and do not leave any rags or paper towels in the engine bay.

If there is a lot of oil leaking from the engine, driving the vehicle will risk damaging the engine or causing it to catch fire.

Until the oil leak has been repaired, you should not drive in a manner that will cause excessive heat build up. Oil

can catch fire if it comes into contact with red hot exhaust manifolds or turbo housings.

4.5 Fuel smell

On modern vehicles with fuel-injected engines you should never be able to smell petrol (gasoline) or diesel unless there is a fault. If you drive an older vehicle that has carburettors or a manual choke, petrol smells are common, and not necessarily an indication of a significant problem. The fuel systems on modern vehicles are sealed, and there should be no smell from inside.

A strong smell of diesel or petrol can be caused by such things as leaking fuel lines, hose connectors, fuel-injector leaks or pressure problems,

Checking fuel-injectors for source of strong petrol or diesel smell.

Check fuel lines for source of strong petrol or diesel smell. (Courtesy CarBasics.co.uk)

or even poor ignition timing. Whatever the cause, chances are that it is pretty serious and requires the attention of an expert mechanic. It is not something that you can just hope will be okay, and not something you should just clean up and then carry on with your journey.

Warning! Turn off the engine, take the keys out of the ignition, and do not use any of the vehicle electrics until the problem is fixed.

Can I still drive the car?
Until you have identified what the problem is and fixed it, you should not drive the car. Leaking fuel has the potential to ignite and cause a potentially fatal incident.

Contact your breakdown recovery service or call out a mechanic to identify the problem. He should be the person to tell you whether the car is safe to drive.

4.6 Rotten egg smell

The most likely cause of this smell is the catalytic converter, and it is a popular misconception that when you can smell rotten eggs it means that it needs changing.

The catalytic converter is designed to convert toxic chemicals into less harmful substances via an internal chemical reaction. However, this chemical reaction will also convert any sulphur in the petrol or diesel into hydrogen sulphide, and this is what the rotten egg smell is. So, this smell will

Catalytic converter – rotten egg smell caused by sulphur in fuel. (Courtesy CarBasics.co.uk)

only occur when the catalytic converter is actually working well – not when it is failing. In fact, a failing catalytic converter will not be performing its chemical reaction effectively and will not be producing any hydrogen sulphide.

If you notice the smell more when starting the car in the morning, or especially after fast accelerating, there is probably no problem and the smell should soon go away. However, cars are not designed to be smelly all the time, and a constant smell of rotten eggs is an indicator that there is something wrong with the fuel mixture of the vehicle. You will need to take your car to your local dealership and have the problem checked out.

The reason people think that the rotten egg smell means the car failing is because the underlying fault with the fuelling *will* eventually result

in the catalytic converter failing – the two problems always seem to come together. Fixing the fuelling problem should remedy the bad egg smell, and also help the catalytic converter last a long time.

Can I still drive the car?
Yes, you can continue to drive the car, but if you do not have the underlying fuelling problem checked then you will definitely eventually need a new catalytic converter.

It may only be a sensor that is causing the fuelling problem. Having that checked and changed will probably cost a lot less than a new catalytic converter.

Tip Consider changing to a low-sulphur fuel instead of your usual stuff and see if the problem smells go away.

five

Leaking liquids

5.1 Oil leaking from gearbox

If you think your car has a gearbox (transmission unit) oil leak, this section will help you confirm where it is coming from, and advise you what to do.

Gearbox oil usually smells more than engine oil – it can be quite distinctive. It is also usually lighter in colour and less thick than engine oil. Check the gearbox oil level. This procedure will not be outlined in the car's user manual, so you will need either a workshop manual specific to your vehicle, or do a search online for more advice. If the level is low, get it topped-up with the correct oil. Again, this information will be in your workshop manual or available online.

Check under the car to see where any oil drips are forming. Remember their location, then give the area a thorough wipe down so you can trace where the gearbox leak is coming from. Common places for transmission leaks

are the driveshaft seals, prop shaft seals, differential seals, end housing and bell housing seals.

Many gearbox oil leaks can be rectified by replacing specific gearbox seals, which can involve much stripping down of the gearbox and associated components. You need a good level of mechanical skill and a good set of tools to perform most kinds of gearbox repair. It may be better to get the fault diagnosed by a good mechanic, and perhaps have them perform the work and give you a good warranty on the repair.

Can I still drive the car?

As with any part of the car that is supposed to contain oil, you should not drive it unless there is sufficient lubrication in the gearbox. A gearbox without any oil in it will fail, and the garage cost for repairing it will be very high, as it will either need the gearbox to be removed and the damaged parts repaired, or a whole new gearbox.

Identifying a leak from the gearbox beneath the car. (Courtesy CarBasics.co.uk)

A typical plastic undertray beneath the engine: it has to be removed before inspection is possible.

Not advisable, unless the leak is tiny, but keeping the gearbox topped up with the correct oil until you can get it repaired may be okay, but it is possible that the internals of the gearbox were damaged whilst it was low on oil.

Be warned: if you continue to ignore a gearbox oil leak, you are also running the risk of the clutch needing to be replaced. If oil is leaking from the gearbox onto the clutch, pretty soon the clutch will stop working and will need replacing.

Gearbox oil leak building up and dripping
from the clutch bellhousing.

5.2 Oil leaking from sump gasket/
plug

A leaking sump (oil pan) gasket or sump
plug can be identified by oil on the road
surface underneath the car, directly
under the middle of the engine, unless
there is an engine undertray.

The sump is basically the pan that
fits to the bottom of the engine, and it
is full of engine oil. The sump gasket
makes the seal between the bottom of
the engine and the sump, and over time
it can start to let oil pass through, and
will then need to be changed.

Many modern vehicles are fitted
with an engine undertray. These prevent
you from seeing the bottom of the
engine until they are removed. They are
normally held in place by a few fixings,
and are quite easy to remove from
underneath the car.

The sump plug is located at the
lowest point of the sump pan. It is
used to drain the engine oil during
an oil change. Many sump plugs are
fitted with 'single use' washers to seal
the plug and, if fitted, these should be
renewed at each oil change and not
be re-used. Oil leaking from the sump
gasket or sump plug can usually be
rectified by fitting a new sump gasket or
fitting a new sump plug sealing washer.

If you want to undertake this work
yourself, it is recommended that you

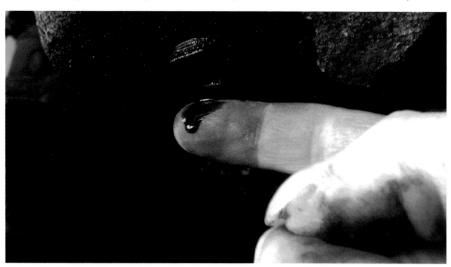

Identifying oil leaking from sump plug. (Courtesy CarBasics.co.uk)

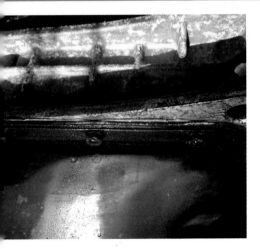

Identifying oil leaking from around the
engine sump gasket.

Check for oil leaks coming from around the
engine oil filter. (Courtesy CarBasics.co.uk)

purchase a workshop manual for the
vehicle so you know exactly what to
do, what type of oil to use, and how
much oil the engine holds. The parts
are readily available from your local car
parts shop or online, and are relatively
cheap.

Whilst changing the sump gasket, it
is recommended that you also take the
opportunity to change the engine oil and
oil filter too, as you will have to drain the
engine oil anyway.

Alternatively, you can get a garage
to perform the work for you. But do
ensure that they use good quality parts,
and that the work carries a guarantee.

Can I still drive the car?
Yes, providing that the leak is small and
the engine always has sufficient oil.
However, leaks tend to get worse with
time!

5.3 Oil leaking from head gasket

As head gaskets become old they
can leak oil. If you find oil leaking from
between the head and the engine

block, this will most likely be the result
of a head gasket failure, and the head
gasket will need to be replaced.

You must also be aware that if the
vehicle has had any engine overheating
problems, the oil leak might be a result
of the head becoming warped and no
longer sitting correctly on the engine
block. This type of fault will require the
head to be repaired or replaced, as well
as a new head gasket.

You need a good level of
mechanical skill and a good set of tools
to perform a head gasket change,
so consider having the repair work
undertaken by a reputable mechanic.
They will also be able to inspect the
engine for signs of wear or damage
and advise you accordingly.

If the underside of the oil filler
cap has yellow sludge on it, this is
an indication of the aforementioned
problems with the engine, and you
should seek expert advice.

Can I still drive the car?
Yes, providing that the engine has
sufficient oil in it and that it is in good

Checking inside the oil filler cap for signs of head gasket failure: this seems okay.

condition, ie there are no signs of water leaking into the oil. There should be no problems with driving the vehicle, as the leak should be quite slow and would appear to be leaking externally and not internally.

Ensure that the engine oil level is checked regularly and topped up if necessary. You should also regularly clean off any excess oil and not allow it to build up in any areas, especially around any heat sources such as turbo housings or exhaust manifolds.

If you feel that the oil leaking from the gasket has occurred as a result of an overheated engine and that the engine has a warped cylinder head, consider getting this repair done quickly. Running a vehicle with a warped head will cause significant damage to other parts of the engine, and will result in the

This oil filler cap shows signs of head gasket or head failure: a creamy sludge deposit.

car needing more than a cylinder head and head gasket replaced.

Oil leak tips
If you are having trouble identifying where an oil leak is coming from, here's a quick tip to help you track it down. Once you have cleaned off all the excess oil from the area, apply a light dusting of lightweight white powder, such as talcum powder, or even foot powder, to the area. Any oil that crosses the area will leave a trail, and you can identify where it is coming from. Also, the powder will soak up the oil and assist in its removal. You may need to carry out this process a number of times to find really tricky leaks.

5.4 Brake fluid leaking from brake lines or hoses

If you think your car has a brake fluid leak from a brake line or hose, this section will help to confirm where it is coming from, and advise what to do.
When new, brake fluid has very little smell and is quite clear, with just a slight

A fluid stain on the ground behind a wheel indicates a brake fluid leak. (Courtesy CarBasics.co.uk)

Inspecting front brake hoses for signs of wear or damage.

Inspecting brake lines for signs of damage or corrosion. (Courtesy CarBasics.co.uk)

Badly-corroded brake lines like this will need to be completely replaced with new examples.

yellow tinge. As it ages it starts to turn a smoky brown colour.

Fluid stains on the ground behind any of the wheels are the best indicator that there is a leak related to that wheel.

Check the brake fluid level to ascertain how much fluid has been lost, and top up to the required level. You may need to jack up the car and remove the wheel in order to view where the leak is coming from.

Caution! Work in a safe manner and always use axle stands if you need to work underneath the car.

If you cannot clearly identify where the brake fluid is leaking from, you may need to wipe off the suspect area with a cloth and pump the brake pedal to try and force the brake fluid out of the leaking part. Make sure you have refilled the brake fluid reservoir before pumping the brake pedal. Do not knock or start the car if it is on an axle stand.

Leaking brake lines or hoses cannot be repaired, they must be replaced urgently. You will need a good level of mechanical skill and a good set of tools to perform any work on the braking system. You may want to consider having the repair work undertaken by a reputable mechanic, as any mistakes could result in you driving a vehicle with faulty or no brakes.

Can I still drive the car?
Beyond the journey to a local garage for repair, no. Driving a vehicle with damaged/faulty brake hoses puts you and others at serious risk of an accident. If the faulty part completely fails, you may be left with no brakes and unable to stop the vehicle safely.

5.5 Brake fluid leaking from a brake calliper or brake drum

If you think your car has a leak from a brake calliper or brake drum, this section will help you to confirm where the leak is coming from, and advise what to do.

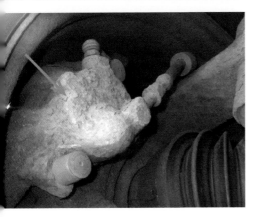

Checking behind the wheel for signs of
brake fluid leaking from the brake calliper.

When new, brake fluid has very
little smell and is quite clear with a slight
yellow tinge. As it ages it starts to go a
smoky brown colour.

Fluid stains on the ground behind
any of the wheels are the best indicator
of a leak related to that wheel. Check
the brake fluid level to ascertain how
much fluid has been lost, and top up to
the required level.

You may need to jack up the car
and remove the wheel, in order to see
where the leak is coming from.

Caution! Make sure you work
safely, and use axle stands if you need
to work underneath the car.

If you cannot clearly identify where
the brake fluid is leaking from, wipe
off the suspect area with a cloth and
pump the brake pedals to try and force
the brake fluid out of the leaking part.
Make sure you have refilled the brake
fluid reservoir before pumping the brake
pedal. Do not knock or start the car if it
is on an axle stand.

Inspecting rear callipers for signs of a brake
fluid leak.

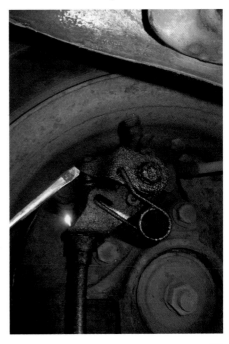

**This rear calliper is showing signs of a brake
fluid leak.**

Leaks that come from brake callipers or drums are usually caused by internal piston seals getting old and worn, allowing brake fluid to pass over them and seep out. Callipers and wheel cylinders can usually be completely replaced or repaired.

Can I still drive the car?

Beyond the journey to a local garage for repair, no. Driving any vehicle with damaged or faulty brake components puts you and others at serious risk of an accident. If the faulty part completely fails, you could be left with no brakes and no method of stopping the vehicle safely.

5.6 Coolant leaking from radiator/engine hose

If you identify engine coolant leaking from the radiator or a coolant hose, the first thing to do is stop the car and check the amount of coolant remaining in the engine. Turn off the engine and check the coolant level at the expansion tank – it should be between the 'min' and 'max' marks shown on the outside.

Depending on the type and size of the leak, you will either need to replace the faulty part or get it repaired. There are products to repair such leaks, available from most car parts shops and some garages. For coolant leaks from pipes and hoses, you can purchase 'emergency repair tape' products: self-amalgamating tapes that wrap around the pipe and stop the leak. For leaks from radiators, you can purchase products like Radweld or Stop Leak that are poured into the cooling system via the expansion tank or radiator cap. As

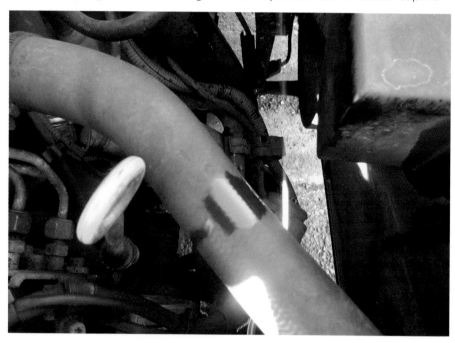

Check hoses for signs of coolant leak like this. (Courtesy CarBasics.co.uk)

Looking down through an engine bay: coolant on road caused by a radiator leak.

A large coolant loss may be the result by a loose water hose, which can be refitted.

the engine runs, they will be pumped around the cooling system to where the fault is and block it when they contact outside air.

The latter type of repair can last a long time, and is often referred to as permanent. The products are cost effective and relatively easy to use by anyone.

Can I still drive the car?
Only if the leak is only very small and you can ensure that the engine will not run low on coolant. It is essential that you keep a close eye on the engine temperature gauge and do not let the engine overheat.

It is recommended that damaged or faulty hoses be replaced as soon as possible, even if the leak has seemingly stopped.

Tip If you have a journey to complete, make sure that you carry a large bottle of water to top up the cooling system.

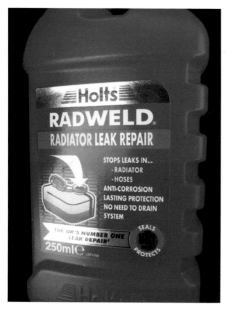

Typical product for repairing leaks in radiators and hoses. (Courtesy CarBasics. co.uk)

Adding leak repair to the expansion tank. (Courtesy CarBasics.co.uk)

six
Exhaust problems

6.1 White smoke coming from the exhaust

White smoke coming from the exhaust is usually caused by water passing through the exhaust system and turning into steam. It's common to have a small amount of white smoke when first starting the car, or in cold weather. This is quite normal and nothing to worry about, but there should be no nasty odours or burning smells.

If there is lots of white smoke billowing from the exhaust (for example, your car looks like a steam train), immediately stop the car and turn off the engine. If you do not, catastrophic damage can occur to the engine.

The most common cause of this symptom is a failed cylinder head gasket or warped head, which must be repaired before the car can be used again. Call your breakdown service or local garage and get the car towed somewhere for the problem to be determined and repaired.

Can I still drive the car?
It is not recommended, because if you do, the engine will not last long. Even if you top up the engine's cooling system with water to prevent overheating, damage will still occur as the water will cross the damaged head gasket and run into the engine oil and cylinders.

6.2 Blue smoke coming from the exhaust

Blue/grey smoke from the exhaust indicates that engine oil is passing the piston rings or valve guides, being burned, and exiting through the exhaust. You may notice that the smoke has a burnt smell to it, different from the normal exhaust smell.

When the engine is working correctly, it should not burn noticeable amount of oil. Large plumes of blue smoke indicate a problem that needs to be looked at immediately, no matter how new or old your vehicle. Small amounts of blue smoke on a high-mileage older car indicate a less immediate, probably wear-related problem. On a newer car, however, this symptom needs to be investigated as soon as possible.

First check the engine oil level and see how much oil has been lost. If you feel it is an age and wear related problem, keep the engine oil topped up to the correct level until the fault has been repaired.

If you feel the problem is not age related, and are concerned that an engine component has failed, you shouldn't drive the car until the problem has been thoroughly investigated. This is definitely the case if your car has lost a lot of engine oil in a very short space of time.

Can I still drive the car?
If the exhaust pipe is emitting large plumes of blue smoke, stop the car straight away and contact your breakdown service or local garage. They may want to tow/trailer it somewhere for further inspection and repair.

If you continue to drive the car in this condition, you could cause terminal damage to the engine.

A small amount of blue smoke on older cars is quite common as the internal engine components wear through use and allow oil to pass. This is more likely a wear-related problem, and although it still needs to be addressed, you should still be able to drive the car as long as you keep a constant close eye on the engine oil level and keep it topped up.

6.3 Exhaust is leaking

A hole in the exhaust may not necessarily mean that you need a replacement exhaust or component. You can easily repair small holes yourself, so won't need to take your car to the garage. There are products available designed to repair small holes.

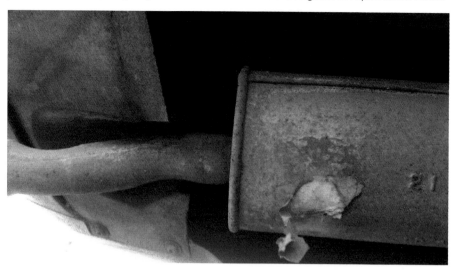

Failed repair of a rear silencer hole caused by corrosion.

Exhaust leaks can occur at loose joints. Try retightening clamps. (Courtesy CarBasics.co.uk)

They make a good low-cost option, and are easy to use.

If you don't repair exhaust holes, they will quickly get worse, resulting in you having to get the exhaust replaced. Holes in the exhaust are not only noisy, they also affect the fuel economy of the car.

Caution! Do not work on a hot exhaust due to risk of burns. Always let the vehicle exhaust cool sufficiently before you commence work on it.

The type of product you use to undertake the repair will depend on the location or size of the hole. The two product types are 'exhaust putty' and 'exhaust bandage.' The exhaust putty is normally used on smaller holes or in areas where exhaust bandage cannot be fixed, such as in a corner. Exhaust

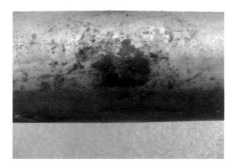

Hole in exhaust pipe highlighted by soot build-up around the outside.

bandage is normally used in easy to access, relatively flat areas.

Can I still drive the car?
Providing that no part of the exhaust system is about to drop off, yes, you

Bandage repair product for repairing exhausts. (Courtesy CarBasics.co.uk)

Bandage repair product used to repair hole in exhaust. (Courtesy CarBasics.co.uk)

Typical putty repair product for repairing smaller holes in exhaust systems.

Exhaust putty product being applied to hole. (Courtesy CarBasics.co.uk)

can still drive the car until the faulty part is repaired or replaced. You may notice that your car uses more fuel whilst the exhaust is leaking, but efficiency should improve once the problem has been rectified.

6.4 Part of the exhaust has come off

Damage can occur to any exhaust system. They are prone to rotting and falling to pieces, and sometimes can get hit or caught on things beneath the car and break off. Clearly if this does happen, you are going to need to get the car repaired straight away. If you have breakdown cover, you do have the option of calling out your provider to assess what can be done. They may be able to get the car going.

Caution! If you smell exhaust fumes inside the car stop immediately and summon help.

Can I still drive the car?

Normally, yes, but only if there are no parts hanging off the car and dragging on the road. Take the car straight home or to a local exhaust specialist. It will be very noisy and you might feel that the car has less power, but driving it a short distance to get it repaired should not cause any damage.

If any of the remaining parts are at risk of coming off whilst you are driving, you will need to remove them or secure them, so that they will not cause a hazard to other road users and not damage your car further.

seven

Windscreen

7.1 Windscreen has cracked

If the windscreen becomes cracked whilst driving, get it replaced as soon as possible. This can normally be done through your insurers for a small cost.

A small chip in the windscreen can be repaired using many of the readily available windscreen chip repair kits.

The question regarding large windscreen cracks is, "can I still drive the vehicle?" Even if you have a really big crack in the windscreen, it is highly unlikely that the windscreen is going to break and fall onto you. Because of the way that modern windscreens are manufactured, they are designed to remain intact. Think of it this way: it is said that with modern cars the windscreen can comprise 30 per cent of the vehicle's overall structural strength. In the event of a hard collision or the car rollling onto its roof, the windscreen will be providing 30 per cent of the vehicle's strength.

Can I still drive the car?
On modern vehicles, providing that the crack is not affecting your visibility, you should be okay to drive short distances until the repair is undertaken.

Caution! From a legal perspective, if you cannot confidently prove that your driving visibility is not affected, you should not drive – it could be classed as a driving offence if you are stopped by the police.

Concerns about driving the car whilst awaiting repair are unfounded. Modern windscreen design means it should be okay to drive, providing you drive appropriately. However, for your peace of mind, check with your insurer that the vehicle is fully insured until the repair can be made.

7.2 Windscreen wipers will not work

If the windscreen wipers stop working,

get them fixed immediately. First check the fusebox to see if the relevant fuse has blown. If it has, change it for a new one of the same value. The car's user manual will tell you the relevant fuse number and location.

If the windscreen wiper fuse keeps blowing, this indicates another problem. The most likely cause will be a seized wiper motor or wiper mechanism which may need to be repaired or replaced. You could try giving the wiper mechanism a spray with a liquid lubricant such as WD40 to see if this solves the problem.

Caution! Do not operate the windscreen wipers when you or someone else is inspecting the wiper mechanism.

If the fault does not appear to be mechanical, the vehicle will need to be looked at by a professional auto-electrician.

Can I still drive the car?
It is a motoring offence to drive your vehicle with defective windscreen wipers, so it should not be driven until they are fixed.

If you are away from home and cannot fix the problem yourself, consider contacting a breakdown service to assess the problem. As the fault is mechanical and renders the car unroadworthy, they should be able to help.

7.3 Windscreen washers won't work

If the windscreen washers stop working, get them fixed immediately.

First top up the washer bottle and test them again. If they are still not working, check the fusebox to see if the relevant fuse has blown. If it has, change it for a new one of the same value. The car's user manual will tell you the relevant fuse number and location.

Washer jets that are not working can cause serious visibility problems.

If the windscreen washer jets are not working, first top up the washer bottle.

If the washer jets are still not working, listen to see if you can hear the pump running when the washer switch is operated. If you can't hear the pump and the fuse is okay, you can pretty much assume that the pump has failed and will need to be replaced. Make sure you have checked the wiring to the washer jet pump before you get it changed.

If you can hear the pump working and there is sufficient fluid In the washer bottle, there may be a blocked washer jets or a blocked pipe that will need to be cleared/cleaned.

Can I still drive the car?
It is a motoring offence to drive your vehicle with defective windscreen washer jets, so it should not be driven until they are fixed.

Please note that it is also a motoring offence to drive with an empty windscreen washer bottle, and it is always a good idea to keep a bottle of water in the car.

eight
Engine

8.1 Engine has cut out when driving

The engine should not just cut out without any warning – normally you would have a warning light or lights appear. If the engine has cut out without any warning, there are a few simple checks that you can perform to dismiss or confirm the most likely problems.

First check that you have not run

If the engine cuts out, check battery terminals are in place. (Courtesy CarBasics.co.uk)

Ensure that the battery terminals are tightly in place and cannot work loose.

out of fuel. Make sure you are confident that the car actually has fuel. A faulty fuel gauge could wrongly indicate that your car has fuel.

Check that the battery terminals are securely in place. Loss of vehicle power can be caused by a battery terminal vibrating loose or not being refitted correctly.

Caution! Do not short the positive terminal to earth (ground) with the tool you are using.

Another consideration is that your car may have a blocked fuel filter or a failed fuel pump. In this instance, when attempting to start the car the engine will turn over, but will not start.

If you have dismissed a fuelling or

battery fault, contact your breakdown service and have them investigate the problem further.

8.2 Car has limited power when driving

If you are driving along and the car seems to have very little power when you accelerate, it may be that the ECU (electronic control unit) has switched itself into what is commonly referred to as 'limp home mode.' This will usually be accompanied by the illumination of an engine warning light.

The purpose of limp home mode is to reduce engine power and protect the engine in the event that the ECU has identified a fault that could be damaging.

It is very common to experience this problem when the engine would normally begin to deliver the most power – for example, a turbo diesel accelerating quickly from low engine speed, and at the point where the turbo would normally be working fully (say between 2000-2500rpm). Here, the ECU reduces the engine output and you feel a substantial reduction in engine power.

Nowadays, modern cars have so many sensors sending information to the ECU that it can be virtually impossible to know what is wrong without the car undergoing a professional diagnostic check.

Can I still drive the car?
Providing that the car seems okay under low-load conditions, ie accelerating lightly and not travelling at high or demanding speeds, it should be okay to drive short distances until the fault is repaired.

If you experience any other symptoms, such as frequent stalling or juddering, then consider not using the

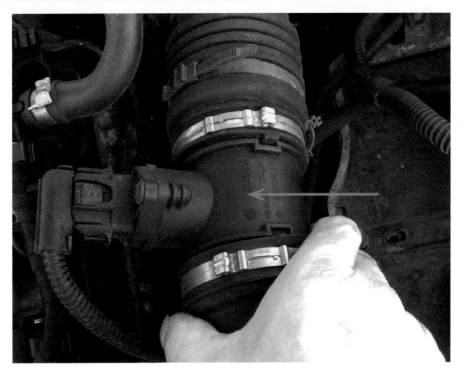

A very common cause of loss of power is the air mass meter. (Courtesy CarBasics.co.uk)

car until the fault has been investigated, as it may cause further damage to the engine.

8.3 Engine overheating

If the engine is overheating, stop and turn it off as soon as possible to investigate the cause. Failing to act promptly can cause catastrophic damage to the engine.

The first thing to check is whether there is an engine coolant leak, and that there is enough coolant in the cooling system. Do this by checking around and under the car for any signs of water. Check that the coolant level is between the 'min' and 'max' marks on the expansion tank.

If there are signs of a water leak or a large loss of engine coolant, investigate this further, as this is the most likely cause of the engine overheating. Topping up the coolant and repairing any leaks with an emergency hose repair or stop-leak product may solve the problem, and allow you to drive the car again. These are available from car spares shops and some fuel filling stations/supermarkets (see chapter 5).

If there is no loss of water and no obvious leak, the radiator fan may not be operating and thus not assisting with cooling the engine. This will be particularly evident in hotter weather. Check whether the radiator fan fuse has blown, and that the wiring to the radiator fan is still intact.

If you cannot identify any of the faults mentioned, assume that there

At any sign of engine overheating, turn it off and check coolant level in expansion tank.

is a more serious reason for the engine overheating. Have it looked at immediately by your breakdown service or a local garage.

Can I still drive the car?
If you cannot find out what is causing the engine to overheat, you shouldn't drive the car until the fault has been identified and rectified.

If the overheating is being caused by a leak or loss of engine coolant, fix the leak, top up the water, and keep a very close eye on it. Overheating can cause catastrophic and very costly damage to the engine.

If you really do need to continue your journey, a good tip is to turn the car interior heating system to hot

and full fan. This may help remove some of the heat from the engine's cooling system, reducing the engine temperature.

Caution! Removing the expansion tank cap on a hot or overheating engine can put you at risk of being scalded from escaping steam. If you do have to remove the cap in this situation, put a heavy cloth over it to protect yourself before you unscrew it.

8.4 Hissing noise/steam coming from under bonnet

This will most likely be water escaping from the engine's cooling system due to a leak. Stop the car immediately and

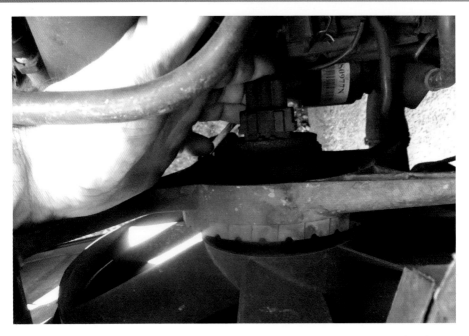

Inspect radiator fan wiring and connectors. A non-operative fan will cause overheating.

Hissing or steam from under the bonnet? Check hoses for water leaks.

turn off the engine. A loss of engine coolant can cause it to overheat, which can cause catastrophic and very costly damage.

Check around and under the car for any signs of water, and check the coolant level, topping up if necessary. On occasion, it has been known for water pipes to come loose, and refitting them can solve the problem. You may need a screwdriver to refit the pipe clamp.

More commonly, the leak will be coming from either a hole in a water pipe or from the radiator. You may be able to fix this by refilling the coolant and repairing the leak with an emergency hose repair or stop-leak product.

If you are not able to repair the leak yourself, consider contacting your breakdown service.

Can I still drive the car?
See section 8.3.

nine
Lights & indicators

9.1 Broken headlight/taillight

If a headlight or taillight bulb fails, get it replaced as soon as possible. It is recommended that you always carry a spare set of bulbs in the car at all times, and make regular checks on bulb operation. The car's user manual may outline the procedures for changing headlight and taillight bulbs.

A broken lens on a headlight or taillight should be repaired or replaced as soon as possible.

With regard to headlight lenses and driving offences, take the following into consideration. Any faulty part of the car's bodywork that can cause damage to a pedestrian can be classed as a driving offence: sharp glass or plastic on a broken headlight lens, for example. Any part of the car that is faulty and causes a hazard to other road users can be classed as a driving offence – for example, a headlight lens repaired with clear tape that dazzles oncoming drivers.

Broken headlights require repair or replacement, and can cause bulbs to fail.

Although you may choose to temporarily cover the headlight lens, you must understand that the lens will no longer be working in the correct manner. Headlight lenses are designed to shine light in a certain direction, where the driver needs it and away from other road users.

With regard to taillight lenses, if any

part of it does not shine in the correct colour you are committing a driving offence. So, a red brakelight segment with the inside bulb shining through a crack can be classed as an offence.

If your car has a cracked lens on one of the rear lights, you can purchase lens repair tape. It comes in clear, amber and red colours, is very easy to apply, and is available from most large car spares shops. As long as the tape is covering the damaged part completely, you should no longer be causing a road traffic offence, and it will also prevent any moisture getting in and blowing the bulb.

Can I still drive the car?
If your car has a broken rear lens and you've fixed it with repair tape, you should be okay to use the car.

With a broken headlight lens, if you do not tape it up then the bulb will be exposed to moisture and debris, and will fail quite quickly. This will make you in breach of another driving law.

From a driving offence perspective, regarding damaged headlight lenses, review this chapter thoroughly and make the appropriate choice yourself based on the damage to the car.

Cracked rear light. This can be repaired using lens repair tape.

Lens repair tape is available in different colours.

ten
Brakes

10.1 Steering wheel vibration when braking

If experiencing vibration through the steering wheel when applying the brakes, you have a brake fault at the front of the vehicle. If experiencing vibration through the steering wheel all the time or when you are not applying the brakes, this will be a different problem, and you will need to explore other sections of this book.

The most common cause of vibration under braking only is a warped brake disc at the front of the car. You can test for this yourself by jacking up the car and rotating each wheel individually by hand. A good brake disc will rotate freely without any problems, with no signs of dragging. A warped disc will sound as though it is dragging at a certain point in its revolution, and you should feel more resistance at that point.

Another quick check is to see if

Identifying a warped disc by checking the wheel for excessive heat build-up.

one wheel is hotter than the others. The hotter side should be the one that is warped.

Caution! Take care not to burn yourself on hot brake parts – you should be able to feel a temperature difference by just feeling the wheel itself. Also, take note of any burning smell that may be coming from the brake pads on the warped side.

Get the faulty brake disc replaced as soon as possible. Have both front discs and pads renewed at the same time.

Can I still drive the car?
Every time you brake, the vibration will be putting more strain on the other suspension and steering components, causing them to wear out sooner. Therefore, although you should be okay to drive the car, not changing the faulty part could end up costing you more in the long run.

If you do need to drive a car with a warped front brake disc, you will need to alter your driving style accordingly to minimise heat build up and reduce the vibrations the car components experience. This can be done by avoiding hard braking, and braking slower/earlier than you normally would.

10.2 Handbrake not holding car stationary

When you apply the handbrake, the (usually) rear brakes of the car should be locked and there should be no movement at all. If the handbrake is not holding the vehicle's weight then there is a fault that needs to be investigated.

Many modern cars are now fitted with electronic parking brakes (EPB) that are controlled by operating a switch to engage and disengage them. If you have one of these systems fitted to the car and there is a fault with it, it is recommended that you take the car to a garage for a diagnostic check.

More commonly, the handbrake will be operated by a lever between the front seats that, when operated, pulls cables underneath the car that put the rear brakes on. Sometimes these cables can stretch or snap and prevent the handbrake from working. If the handbrake is not working at all, then it is most likely that one of these cables has snapped and will need to be replaced. If the handbrake is working a little, then it is most likely that one of the cables has stretched and will need to be adjusted.

Adjusting or changing a handbrake

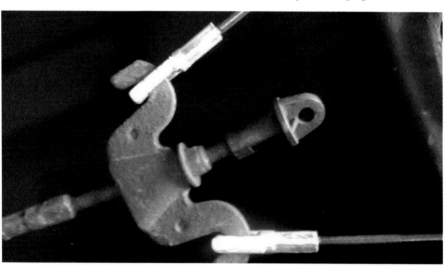

Typical arrangement allowing adjustment of handbrake cables underneath car.

cable will not usually be outlined in the car user manual, so if it is a job you wish to do yourself you may need to purchase a workshop manual, or have a look online for information.

The handbrakes on many modern vehicles can be adjusted from inside the vehicle by removing the gaiter around the lever and making an adjustment to the mechanism (see workshop manual or internet).

If your car's handbrake cable is adjusted from beneath the vehicle, you can trace the handbrake cables to the middle of the car, where they all meet – the main one from the front of the car, and two smaller ones that go to each wheel. They meet together in a 'Y' shape, and it is at this point the handbrake can be adjusted. There will be a length of thread with a nut on it – this nut will alter the amount of distance the handbrake cable has to be moved before the rear brakes come on. With the handbrake off, turn the nut clockwise to tighten the slack from the rear cables. Adjust it by only a few turns, then apply the handbrake and see if the rear wheels lock. You may need to make the adjustment a few times to get it exactly right. Remember not to over-tighten the handbrake adjuster, as this can cause the brakes to bind and the cable to stretch or snap.

If the handbrake remains inefficient after adjustment, consider that rear brake shoes or discs may need changing, or that one of the handbrake cables has stretched or snapped and will need to be changed.

With a snapped brake cable, you can either change all three sections or just the piece that has broken. The parts don't all have to be new for the handbrake mechanism to work correctly.

Replacing a handbrake cable is relatively easy. With the handbrake in the off position, the cables should unhook from any holders along the chassis. A workshop manual will make the job even easier, and the cost of it and the new parts should still be less than paying someone else do the work.

Caution! Performing any work underneath your car can be dangerous, and you must ensure that the car is secure and will not move whilst the work is being carried out. Make good use of axle stands, and chock the wheels firmly before going underneath.

Can I still drive the car?

You will still be able to drive temporarily, providing there are no bits of brake cable hanging off the underside of the car. You will, however, have to ensure that you can drive the car safely without the use of a handbrake. For example, are you confident and practised enough to perform hill starts using only the brake pedal and clutch, without the car rolling backwards and hitting someone? If the answer to this is no, then you should not be driving the car until it has been repaired.

You will also need to ensure there is a safe place to park the car when you reach your destination. You will have to leave the vehicle in gear to prevent it from rolling, so park it on a flat surface.

Tip If you do have to park on an incline and choose to leave the car in the relevant gear, it is suggested that you turn the front wheels into the kerb with the nose of the car pointing downhill. This may help to prevent the car from moving in the unlikely event of slipping out of gear, and will also help relieve some of the pressure on the gearbox. When facing downhill, the front wheels should be turned slightly towards the kerb with the weight of the vehicle touching the kerb. When facing uphill, the front wheels should be turned slightly away from the kerb, letting the vehicle roll back slightly so it touches the kerb. If you drive an automatic, leave the vehicle in P (park).

Tip If you do have wheel chocks available, it is highly recommended that you make use of them.

Caution! If your car has a failed handbrake cable, never leave passengers in the car unattended.

10.3 Wheel locking under braking

Wheels on cars should not lock up when the brakes are applied – it is very dangerous, and whilst the car is skidding it is out of control.

Most modern cars are fitted with anti-lock braking systems (ABS) that should prevent the wheels from locking. They are designed to reduce braking distances and also allow you to steer the car around any obstacles whilst braking.

If you have ABS on your car, and you find a wheel is locking under braking, then there is definitely a fault with the system. This may be a faulty wheel sensor or a problem with the ABS control unit. If you experience regular locking up of the brakes, even if your car is not fitted with ABS, you may have a very serious problem with the car's braking system that needs to be investigated immediately.

Ensure the tyres are road legal, that there is sufficient air pressure in them, and that they have plenty of tread.

Can I still drive the car?
Clearly this is not a good situation to be in. A skidding car is one that is out of control, and it is not safe to drive.

Typical ABS sensor. The wheels should not lock up if the ABS is working correctly.

Regular locking of wheels is not a common problem and is very serious. Have the vehicle inspected as a matter of urgency. Contact your breakdown service – it should consider this situation a breakdown, as the car is not safe to drive. If your service cannot identify and rectify the problem, it will probably tow/trailer your car to a garage for further inspection.

10.4 Handbrake locked on/dragging wheel

If your car is fitted with an electronic parking brake (EPB) and the handbrake will not release, there is a fault with the system that will need to be diagnosed by a garage. Many EPB systems are fitted with a manual release mechanism that will disengage the system in the event of a fault. The location and safe use of this manual release should be shown in the user manual.

In very cold weather, a locked handbrake can often be caused by

A seized handbrake cable can be manually released. (Courtesy CarBasics.co.uk)

water that has got into the handbrake cable sleeves and frozen solid. This is more common in older vehicles, and will probably continue to occur until the defective cables have been replaced.

Seized or frozen handbrake cables on rear brakes can often be released manually from underneath the car. At the point where the handbrake cable meets the rear brake there should be a lever that can be forced with a screwdriver, releasing the cable.

If the handbrake cables are functioning normally, there may be a seized rear brake caliper/drum mechanism. You can identify which wheel is seized by jacking up the rear of the car and rotating the wheels by hand. This will have to be done with the handbrake off, so make sure the wheels on the ground are chocked adequately and the vehicle will not move. Once identified, you will need to either have the faulty part replaced or repaired.

Fitting new handbrake cables may be necessary if the handbrake regularly sticks on or drags.

If the rear of your car is fitted with drum brakes, they may need to be stripped and cleaned or parts replaced. Wheel cylinders within drum brakes are a common cause of many faults, but seized springs or adjusters can also be the problem, which a good clean up can often rectify.

If the rear of the car is fitted with disc brakes, a common fault with the caliper is that the surface of the 'sliders' or 'slider pins' becomes pitted by corrosion, preventing free movement and hence brake dragging. The sliders are protected by rubber grommets, and when these perish and split, moisture and road salt get inside and cause damage to the sliding surfaces. You can either fit a new replacement caliper or purchase a caliper repair kit that will include new grommets etc, and clean up the old sliders.

Caution! You will be under the car when you release the handbrake, so make sure the vehicle is in gear and that the wheels are suitably chocked to prevent rolling.

Can I still drive the car?
Until the handbrake has been released, it is not safe to drive the car. Even if you can rotate the rear wheels by applying more engine power, you will cause the rear brakes to overheat causing damage. Also, you are at risk of loosing control of the car whilst driving as the car will not be operating as it has been designed. For example, in poor road conditions the rear wheels can lock up and lose traction, causing the rear of the car to slide out when cornering.

Handbrake tips
If you have time, and the car is in an appropriate location, it may be possible to warm up the handbrake cables with a hair dryer or small electric heater.

Caution! Appropriate safety measures need to be taken when using electrical appliances outdoors to avoid electric shock.

Do not attempt to manually release the handbrake mechanism unless the front wheels are chocked securely and the car is in gear. If you can gain access under the rear of the car without using a jack then this is recommended.

Where possible, to prevent winter freezing of the handbrake cables, spray a water dispersing lubricant like WD40 inside the cables, and cover any openings at each end with petroleum jelly. If this is a continuing problem every time the weather gets cold, it will be best practice to replace both of the handbrake cables with new ones. The inside of the handbrake cables is probably corroded, and the cables will keep seizing and/or eventually break, resulting in no handbrake at all.

Caution! If your car is positioned on a steep incline, do not attempt to manually release the rear brakes. Use the warming-up method with the handbrake on, the car in gear (opposite to the incline), and the wheels chocked. Alternatively, wait until the weather warms and the handbrake cables thaw out.

10.5 Brake pedal feels spongy when depressed

Any change in your car's braking performance or characteristics should be investigated as soon as possible and not ignored. If, when applying the brakes, the brake pedal feels softer than normal, this can be an indication of low brake fluid level or air in the braking system. Braking systems are sealed, and should not have any air in them at all. Air in the system will compress easily (unlike brake fluid) and will have

Check brake fluid level if the foot brake feels spongy: it should be at the maximum mark.

a negative affect on the car's braking ability.

Air can only get into the braking system through a faulty part or due to poor repairs to brake parts. You will need to have all of the air bled out of the braking system to return it to normal working order. You will need a good level of mechanical skills and a good tool kit in order to bleed your car's braking system. Have this work undertaken by a good mechanic, as they may also be able to identify any potential problems.

If the fault returns after having the brake system bled, your car has a faulty part, such as a leaking brake caliper or worn master cylinder. The defective parts will need to be replaced and the system bled again.

Can I still drive the car?

Any vehicle that has a braking fault is potentially dangerous. Before taking the car to be repaired, you must ensure

A brake bleed nipple: these allow air to be bled from the brake system.

A worn master cylinder can let air into the brake system and cause spongy brakes.

there is sufficient brake fluid in the system by topping up, if necessary, and you must be confident that you can drive the distance safely without losing adequate braking performance. If not, you will be committing a driving offence and putting yourself and other road users at risk.

If you are in any doubt about this, you should not drive the car. Have it trailered to the garage or have the work undertaken where it is.

10.6 Brake pedal – excessive travel

Any change in braking performance or characteristics should be investigated as soon as possible. If, when applying your car's brakes, the brake pedal travels further than normal, this is an indication of low brake fluid level or air in the braking system.

The braking system is sealed, and doesn't use up brake fluid over time. Any loss of fluid is a result of a leak that needs to be investigated. Check the brake fluid level and top it up if necessary. After topping up, start the car and pump the brake pedal to see if it returns to its normal feel.

If you are still experiencing excessive brake pedal travel, this may be due to air in the braking system that will need to be bled out. This should be done by a qualified mechanic if you do not have the suitable experience.

Can I still drive the car?
Any vehicle that has a braking fault is potentially dangerous. See 10.5.

10.7 Brake fluid leaking from front brakes

When new, brake fluid has very little smell and is quite clear with a slight yellow tinge. As it ages it starts to go a smoky brown colour.

Fluid stains on the ground behind any of the wheels are the best indicator that there is a leak related to that wheel. Check the brake fluid level to ascertain how much fluid has been lost, and top up to the required level.

You may need to jack up the car and remove the wheel in order to view where the leak is coming from.

Caution! Work in a safe manner, and use axle stands if you need to work underneath the car. The most common places for fluid leaks from the front brakes are the brake caliper, holes in brake hoses or leaking unions.

Often the seals inside the brake caliper can be worn or damaged, causing brake fluid to leak past the pistons. This will require a new brake caliper to be fitted, or new seals in the existing caliper.

Can I still drive the car?
It is not recommended that any vehicle with a leaking braking system is driven, no matter how small the leak. Contact your breakdown service or call out a local garage.

Caution! If the leak seems to be coming from a hose, this is far more dangerous and you absolutely must not drive the car. Although not very

Checking brake hose unions on front brakes for fluid leaks.

Clean dirt from around unions, and check tightness of fitting.

common, damage or wear to a brake hose can result in a sudden loss of brakes, as the damage will worsen quickly, resulting in rapid loss of brake fluid ... and brakes.

10.8 Brake fluid leaking from rear brakes

When new, brake fluid has very little smell and is quite clear with a slight yellow tinge. As it ages it starts to go a smoky brown colour.

Fluid stains on the ground behind any of the wheels are the best indicator that there is brake fluid a leak related to that wheel. Check the brake fluid reservoir to ascertain how much has been lost, and top up to the required level. You may need to jack up the car and remove the wheel to find the leak.

A common drum brake leak is from the hydraulic brake cylinder inside the drum (top).

Brake fluid leaks away from the wheels will be coming from corroded brake lines.

Caution! Follow the usual safety procedures: see section 10.7.

If the rear axle of your car is fitted with disc brakes, the most common place for a brake fluid leak is from the seals inside the brake caliper, or the union of the brake hose with the caliper body.

Often, the seals inside the brake caliper can be worn or damaged and cause brake fluid to leak. See 10.7.

If the rear axle of the car is fitted with drum brakes, the most common places for brake fluid to be leaking from are the brake (slave) cylinder inside the drum, or the union of the hydraulic line with the wheel cylinder.

If the supply of brake fluid to the rear of the car is via metal brake lines, rather than flexible hoses, it is common for them to become corroded and leak over time. Brake fluid stains near

the rear of the car, but away from the wheels, are an indicator of corroded brake lines.

It is recommended that any work on leaking brake cylinders, brake pipes or unions is performed by a qualified mechanic.

Can I still drive the car?
No. You must not drive a vehicle with a leaking braking system, no matter how small the leak appears to be. Contact your breakdown service or call out a local garage.

10.9 Steering pulls to the left/right under braking

When applying the brakes on your car, if it begins to turn to one side or the other then there is a fault that needs to be investigated.

The first thing to check is tyre pressures, and although a car with mismatched tyre pressure should likely have a pull all of the time, it will be more noticeable under braking. Because the pulling can be caused by a number of faults, it is important to eliminate the most obvious things first, so check that the tyres are all the same size too.

If you have any suspicion that the fault is related to tyres, consider switching them to different sides, or moving them from font to rear to see if this eliminates the problem.

Check brake pads and brake discs for wear, especially uneven wear. If you notice that one side is more worn than the other, this indicates uneven braking force being applied. Check for contamination of the brake pads and discs – any oil, grease or lubricant on them will affect their braking capabilities. Any odd wearing on the surface of a brake disc, such as deep grooves within the pad contact area, indicates a fault with the brake pads or the disc itself.

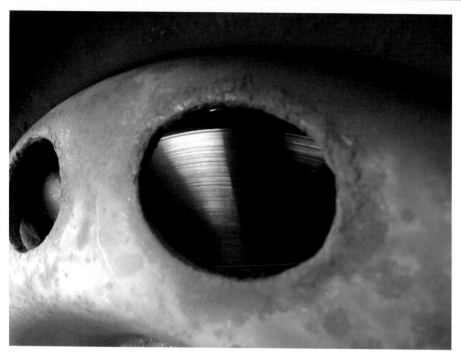

Check your car's brake discs and pads for uneven wear. (Courtesy CarBasics.co.uk)

A brake disc showing uneven wear. This fault can reduce braking force and cause the steering to pull to one side under braking.

Brake pad showing uneven wear, which can reduce braking force and cause the steering to pull to one side under braking.

If you have any suspicion that the brake pads or discs are at fault, they should be changed, in matching pairs, to see if this eliminates the problem.

Another common fault is a sticking brake caliper on the opposite side to the direction of pull. If the car pulls to the left under braking, it may be that the brake caliper on the right is not operating freely and applying less braking force. This requires the fitting of a replacement brake caliper or a repair to the existing one.

Also, consider misalignment of the wheels/suspension, as any fault in this area can be far more evident under braking.

If the cause of the fault is still not evident, you will need to take the car to a brake specialist.

Can I still drive the car?
As long as the pulling to one side is gradual, ie not a sharp or severe snatching, and easily controlled by the steering wheel, you should be okay to drive the car until the repair has been undertaken, but do regard the repair as urgent.

10.10 Brake pedal pulses under heavy braking

The most likely explanation of this is the sensation you experience when the ABS system is operating and you can feel quick pulses through the brake pedal. Braking heavily causes a pulsating feel through the footbrake as the system prevents the wheels from locking and skidding. If this symptom only appears under heavy or emergency braking the ABS is working correctly and there is not a brake fault.

If your car is not fitted with ABS, a pulsating pedal indicates a brake system fault. The most likely cause of this symptom is a warped brake disc or faulty wheel bearing.

You can test for a warped brake disc by jacking up the car and rotating each wheel individually by hand. A good brake disc will allow the wheel to rotate freely without any signs of dragging. A warped disc will sound as though it is dragging at a certain point in the wheel revolution, and you should feel momentary resistance to turning.

Another quick check is to see if one of the wheels is hotter, near its centre, than the other after a drive.

Caution! Take care not to burn yourself. The hotter side will be the one with a warped brake disc. There may also be a burning smell coming from the brake pads on the warped side.

You must get the faulty brake disc replaced as soon as possible. Renew both front discs and pads at the same time to prevent uneven braking.

With regards to a faulty wheel bearing, you can perform the same heat test as for a warped brake disc. If your car makes a humming or grumbling noise that seems to increase or decrease proportionate to vehicle speed, it is most likely a faulty wheel bearing. Refer to chapter 3.3, 'Wheel noises,' for more guidance on failed wheel bearings.

Can I still drive the car?
Yes, you can drive home or to get the car to a garage. Make sure to adjust your driving appropriately, as the car's braking performance will be noticeably reduced.

10.11 Brakes or a wheel getting very hot

If, under normal driving conditions, you find that the brakes at one of the wheels are getting very hot – perhaps you can smell them, especially when outside of the car – then this fault needs to be looked into as soon as possible.

The most common causes of this are either a warped brake disc, a binding caliper or a faulty wheel bearing.

Normally, the overheating will manifest itself on one side of an axle and the faulty side can be found by feeling the wheel with your hand.

Caution! Take care not to burn yourself and, especially, do not touch the disc or pads. Whichever side is the hottest is the side with the fault.

Think about what other symptoms you are experiencing with the car, such as braking noises or pulling to one side. Then, to investigate the fault further, refer to the other sections on braking in this book.

Can I still drive the car?
You should not drive the car until the fault has been investigated thoroughly.

10.12 Electric parking brake (referred to as EPB or e-brake) failure

If the car is fitted with an electronic parking brake (EPB) and it is not functioning correctly, for example will not disengage or re-engage, the most common problems are usually a motor/actuator failure or an electrical switch failure.

A fault with the switch on the dashboard will prevent the system from functioning correctly, so you should check that the relevant fuse has not blown. Your car's handbook will identify the correct fuse and its location.

You may need to take the car to have a professional diagnostic check performed on it. The technician should be able to get the fault codes from the car to help identify what the problem is.

In an emergency, if the EPB will not engage and you need to get out of the car, leave it in gear. If you are on a hill, put it into a gear opposed to the direction you're pointing, ie if facing downhill put the car in reverse, and if facing up hill put the car in first gear. If you drive an automatic, leave the vehicle in P (park). You can also turn the front wheels so that they will be chocked by the kerb.

If the EPB is locked on and will not disengage, or if the car has a flat battery, some models are fitted with a manual handbrake release mechanism. Refer to the car's user handbook and read the section about EPB; it should outline where the manual release is and how to operate it. If it is not in the user manual, search online for information on your specific car.

Most often, the manual or emergency brake release is mounted under a panel in the centre console. Many have a pull-ring on them, and can be operated using tools from the toolkit that was supplied with the car.

Please note that manual release is available only on EPB systems that use a cable to operate rear brake calipers.

eleven
Gearbox & clutch

11.1 Manual gearbox/clutch faults

Cannot select a gear
If you are experiencing problems getting the car into a gear, or a number of gears, there could be a variety of causes.

The first thing to check is that there is sufficient oil in the gearbox. Rule this out first before considering any other possible problems. If the gearbox oil is low, top up and see if the problem has gone. Refer to chapter 5, section 5.1, 'Oil leaking from gearbox,' as gearboxes should not normally need to be topped up.

Another possible cause is that the linkage (not all cars use a linkage) connecting the gearstick to the gearbox needs to be adjusted, or has worn and needs to be repaired. If this linkage has altered slightly due to damage or wear, the gearbox components will not align correctly and you won't be able to select gears easily. In order to rectify

this, the gearbox linkage will need to be inspected for damage or wear.

If you suspect any damage to the underside of the car, a good thing to check whether any heat shields or protective trays have been bent and are fouling the gear selector mechanism. This may just be a matter of bending them back into shape, out of the way of the mechanism.

Removing the plastic surround and gaiter from around the gear stick should allow access to some of the linkage components. Any wear in the gear linkage rods or associated bushes can make it difficult to engage gears. If joints feel very loose and have lots of play in them, they may need to be replaced. Also, check the linkage where it attaches to the gearbox. This may need to be accessed from underneath the car, or through the engine bay. Again, check for worn linkages and joints with lots of play in them. If it looks like these are at fault, they will need to be replaced.

Difficulty selecting gear might be due to a gear linkage problem.

Do not adjust the gear linkage unless you have a certain degree of mechanical skill and a relevant workshop manual. Incorrect adjustment can make gear selection even worse, so if you are at all uncertain perhaps you should have a mechanic undertake the work for you.

Another possible fault is the gearbox synchromesh wear. If you are experiencing problems getting the car into second and third gear, this is often a common cause. Synchromesh faults usually cause the most problems on the gears that are most often used. If you have been experiencing increased difficulty in selecting certain gears, and the car tends to crunch a lot when going into those gears, the gearbox synchromesh may need to

be changed. The main problem with this is that, although the synchromesh is not a large part of the gearbox, replacing the components can be very labour intensive and hence quite costly. However, this can still work out cheaper than a new or reconditioned gearbox.

There is a lot of discussion on the internet regarding changing the gearbox oil to a type that will help with gearbox synchromesh problems and crunchy gear changes. For the cost, this might be something that you should look into further. If your car is under warranty, any gearbox problems should be referred to your car dealer as they may be covered.

Consider also that the clutch may need to be changed. You can experience more and more difficulty

A clutch that needs replacing can make gear selection difficult.

go any faster. You'll see the RPM rise on the rev counter, but gain no speed. This can be more apparent when moving off from stationary, especially if you are pulling a load or have a full car.

If this is happening and you have just had a new clutch fitted, you need take the car straight back to the garage. This could be oil contamination or misalignment of the release bearing/ system.

How to test for a slipping clutch
Drive at a slow speed with the car in a high gear (fourth or fifth) and then accelerate. If the vehicle does not bog down (begin to stall), and engine speed increases with the accelerator pedal, but vehicle speed does not increase, the clutch is slipping.

As most modern vehicles have self-adjusting clutches, there are probably no adjustments that can be made to improve clutch bite, and you need to get the clutch replaced.

Can I still drive the car?
Yes and no. As long as you can engage the gears okay, then the car can be driven. However, the clutch will continue to wear ever faster, and soon the car will be undriveable because you will no longer be able to engage any gears. So it is best to get the clutch changed as soon as possible, before you're left stranded.

Tips for driving with a slipping clutch
These are tips designed to only get you to a garage to get the car fixed.

A slipping clutch could completely fail at any time, which could result in you being stranded or the car being left in a hazardous place. Eventually the clutch will just slip continuously, as it can no longer transfer any power from the engine to the gearbox, as

in selecting gears as the clutch wears. Refer to the next section for advice on how to identify a slipping clutch (indicating severe wear or oil contamination). Unless you have a high level of mechanical skill and a good set of tools, it is recommended that you have the clutch replaced by a garage that provides quality parts and a good level of warranty for your money.

How to identify a slipping clutch
The typical symptom of a slipping clutch is that when you accelerate, and the engine noise increases, the car does not

Typical clutch plate, showing friction material around outside.

there is no friction material remaining on the clutch plate or the friction plate is contaminated. Drive very gently, changing gear with the least amount of acceleration possible, lifting the clutch back up slowly. Try to keep the engine revs as low as possible when changing gear. Try to minimise the number of gear changes you are making, as each gear change will cause further wear.

Car jumps out of gear

If the car is regularly jumping out of gear, there is a fault that needs looking into. This symptom occurs most commonly in higher gears, and usually when decelerating the engine with the clutch engaged.

Often the gearbox can throw itself out of gear when the gear

has not been selected properly, due to a worn or badly adjusted gear selector linkage. You can read more on this in the previous section 'Cannot get gearbox into gear.' A poorly engaged gear can be prone to popping out of engagement as its load changes under deceleration. Rectification will require adjustment or changing of gear linkage (if applicable) parts.

A more serious common cause of the car jumping out of gear is wear within the gearbox. If you drive an older car, or a car that has done a lot of miles, this problem can occur due to wear on gearbox internal parts, most likely syncro hubs and gear selector forks. If this is the cause of the problem, the only solution is to have the gearbox stripped and overhauled, or a replacement gearbox (new, reconditioned or second hand). If you do opt to have a second hand gearbox fitted in order to keep repair costs down, make sure you purchase it from a supplier that will give a good guarantee in case of any problems.

11.2 Automatic gearbox/clutch faults

An automatic gearbox is a very complex component of your vehicle, and usually requires a gearbox expert to diagnose and repair any problems.

The key to keeping the costs down on a car with automatic transmission is ensuring it always has sufficient good quality fluid in it, and investigating even the slightest fault or symptom as soon as possible.

Keeping up with regular service intervals specifically related to the automatic gearbox can save you a lot of money over time, and also helps maintain the value of the vehicle.

On modern vehicles with automatic transmission, there are so many electronics controls and sensors that faults can rarely be identified without a professional diagnostics check.

It really is very important to have any gearbox problems, such as harsh or rough gear changing, or difficulty changing down through the gears, looked into as soon as possible. If you ignore these symptoms, more problems can be caused such as gearbox overheating, which can result in even more repair work.

Automatic gearbox fluid
If you experience any kind of problem with an automatic gearbox, first check the gearbox oil (automatic transmission fluid: ATF) level. A low level of transmission fluid can cause many problems in automatic gearboxes, and it should always be the first thing to check. If the automatic gearbox has a transmission fluid dipstick, check and top up the ATF level via the tube it is located in. Some automatic gearboxes do not have dipsticks, and you will need a workshop manual to find out how to check the level, or take the car to a garage to have it done.

Automatic transmission fluid levels are usually checked when the engine is hot and, often, the dipstick will indicate both hot and cold levels.

When new, automatic transmission fluid is red, so if it is going a brown colour, check whether it's due a change or service. The automatic transmission should also have a filter inside it that should always be changed at the correct intervals.

Also, if the transmission fluid is brown or smells burnt it is definitely time to get the gearbox serviced by having the fluid and filter changed. Overheating of automatic transmission can cause big problems, and the burning smell is a sign of this. Have this looked into as soon as possible. It may just be a case

of the gearbox needing a service, or it could be a bigger problem that needs to be rectified before the transmission fails completely.

Automatic gearbox stuck in park
Most automatic gearbox selectors cannot be taken out of the 'P' (park) position until the driver depresses the brake pedal, presses the shift lever button, and turns the ignition key to the 'on' position. Behind the foot pedal will be a relay/switch which tells the gearbox that the brake pedal is depressed and that the shift can be moved. If there is a fault with the relay or any of the associated wiring, the selector cannot be moved out of 'P.' Check that all of the related fuses and wiring are in working order and not damaged.

A flat battery may cause the gearbox to be locked in the park position. In this instance, you will need to charge or change the car's battery and, unless there is another fault, should then be able to move the selector out of the park position.

Shift lock release
If the car is fitted with a 'shift lock release' mechanism (also referred to as shift lock override), you can operate this to allow you to move the gear selector out of the 'P' position.

You will need to locate the position of the shift lock release mechanism (it may be outlined in the car's user manual, or you can search for information online). Often it is located in close proximity to the gear selector, and operation usually just involves insertion of a screwdriver or car key to move the selector to 'N' (neutral). Sometimes it will have a small cover that you need to first remove before it can be operated.

The shift lock release should not be used constantly. Any underlying fault with the gear shift should be looked into, and the relevant parts repaired or replaced.

Tip To avoid putting unnecessary strain on the gearbox and causing problems in the future, follow these steps when parking the car. Not doing so can cause difficulties with the

selector refusing to move out of the park position:
1) Stop the car fully using the footbrake.
2) Apply the handbrake fully.
3) Put the selector into neutral.
4) Release the footbrake.
5) Put the selector into park position.

twelve
Steering

12.1 Steering pulls to the left/right whilst driving

The most common causes of a car pulling to one side during normal driving are unequal tyre pressures, wheel alignment or worn suspension parts.

Ensure that you have the correct pressure in all of the tyres, and that none has suffered a puncture.

If you have any suspicion that the pulling is related to tyres, consider switching wheels to different sides, or moving them from front to rear, to see if this eliminates the problem. Also check the tyres for uneven tyre wear, as this can indicate where the problem lies. A tyre that is over-inflated will experience more tread wear at the centre of the tread. A tyre that is under-inflated will experience more wear at the edges of the tread.

If you are experiencing heavier tread wear on one edge (inner or outer), this is an indication that the car has a wheel alignment problem, and/or possibly worn suspension components. You will need to take your car to a wheel alignment specialist (usually found at tyre and exhaust centres) which will check and adjust the alignment of the wheels. The specialist will also advise you about any worn parts that are causing the misalignment.

Can I still drive the car?
Yes, you should be okay to drive the car but you should have the fault professionally investigated as soon as possible.

Understand that, although you can control the pulling of the steering by turning the steering wheel slightly in the opposite direction, doing so puts excessive strain on the tyres and suspension parts. It is more cost effective to diagnose and repair the fault early and save on the cost of new tyres, and possibly even suspension parts, too.

12.2 Squealing noise when turning steering wheel

If you hear a screeching or whining noise when you turn the steering wheel, there is most likely a fault with your power steering hydraulic pump or power steering pump drivebelt. The noise will be most apparent when the vehicle is stationary and you turn the steering wheel, at slow speeds, or on full lock. You should not experience this type of noise if the vehicle is fitted with electronic power steering (EPS).

The noise is usually generated by the power steering belt as it slips when put under load. This most commonly happens with age, as the belt stretches over time. A worn/stretched belt should be changed as soon as possible.

The other possible cause of this noise is that the power steering system is low on fluid, or that the pump itself is at fault. First check the power steering fluid level and top up if necessary. If you do not have much mechanical experience, you may want to have the top up carried out by your local garage, as the procedure is not often covered in the car handbook.

Can I still drive the car?

The car can still be driven, but if the belt comes off or snaps, you will suddenly be left without any power steering, and if this happens whilst you are driving it could result in an accident.

If the cause of the noise is low power steering fluid level, driving the vehicle like this could cause damage to the power steering pump, resulting in it needing to be replaced.

The fault will continue to get worse until the necessary parts have been repaired or replaced, and you must be cautious of the potential for abrupt changes in the steering feel whilst driving.

Squealing when on full lock can be caused by a slipping power steering belt.

Checking for a loose power steering belt.

Tip If the power steering system needs to be topped with fluid, find out why, as there may be a leak.

12.3 Steering has become very heavy

Here are some possible causes of the steering becoming heavy:
• Flat tyre. The very first thing that you should do is check that the front

Heavy steering car be caused by low power steering fluid. Check level.

The power steering reservoir will be located in the engine bay. Check and top up if needed.

tyres are fully inflated to the correct pressures. A tyre with low pressure may cause the steering to become heavier. If low pressure is caused by a puncture you to get the tyre repaired or replaced immediately.
• Power steering fluid level low. This may be accompanied by a groaning noise from the power steering pump. Top up the power steering fluid to see if this solves the problem. You'll need to investigate the reason for the loss of fluid, maybe be a leak from the power steering pump or associated pipework.
• Power steering pump failure; a screeching noise on full lock or at start-up can be an indication of a failing power steering pump. Driving with a failing power steering pump can be risky because, if it is seizes, there is a chance that it will snap the drivebelt and cause other problems. You will have to investigate this further.

Check that heavy steering is not caused by a flat tyre or low tyre pressure.

• Power steering drivebelt failure. If the belt has completely snapped and come off, the steering will be very heavy, but there will be no screeching or groaning noises. Note that the power steering drivebelt may also drive other components such as the water pump and air-conditioning compressor.

Caution! Correct operation of the water pump is particularly important as the engine will overheat without it.

• Electronic power steering (EPS) failure. You will probably see a warning light illuminate on the dashboard, indicating complete power steering failure or intermittent loss of power steering. Common EPS failures are the electronic torque sensor and electronic control unit. You can still drive the car, but the steering will be very heavy. The steering wheel is still safely linked directly to the wheels, but there will be no power assistance when steering.

Try turning off the ignition for a few minutes, then restarting the engine and testing the steering again. If the problem goes away, this is only a temporary fix and the fault still needs to be investigated as it may suddenly return.

If the EPS has a city or parking mode that makes steering lighter whilst town driving in traffic or parking, make sure you turn it off for normal driving. These settings make the steering motor work harder to make the steering lighter, and using them continuously can cause problems.

You will need to take the car to a qualified garage to investigate and repair the fault.

Tip If the car has EPS fitted and you keep getting an intermittent power steering fault, make sure that the battery and charging system are working properly. Ensure there are no loose connections at the battery.

thirteen

4x4 problems

Because there are so many different 4x4 and 4WD systems fitted to vehicles, this book cannot be specific about any particular one. This section will try to cover the most common 4x4 problems and provide general solutions and recommendations for maintaining the health of your 4x4 system. For the purposes of this chapter, 4x4 will also refer to 4WD and AWD (All Wheel Drive) systems.

13.1 4x4 oil and oil leaks

Maintaining the health of your 4x4 system is essential, and neglecting regular servicing can cost a lot of money in repairs. Neglecting to act quickly to correct a leak can result in catastrophic damage to transfer boxes, differentials, etc.

Also, do not ignore any 4x4 warning lights that appear on the dashboard, even if they flash on for a brief period and then go out again.

If you are experiencing an oil leak from a 4x4, or suspect that an oil level is low, top up the leaking unit with the correct oil as soon as possible. It is unlikely that the transfer box or differentials will have any method of inspecting oil level inside them. In most cases these units are 'fill to overflow,' meaning it is a case of removing the filler plug and topping up with oil until it begins to flow back out of the filler hole, then refitting the plug.

Keep the system topped up with oil until, as quickly as possible, it can be inspected and repaired by a professional.

You should consider purchasing a workshop manual for the vehicle, as it may help you to diagnose the cause of the leak, and will also help keep your running and repair costs down.

13.2 4x4 noises

If the 4x4 system is making groaning

Maintaining the health of your 4x4 system is crucial for keeping control of running costs.

or grinding noises that you have not experienced before, these should be investigated as soon as possible. The noises may be more evident during cornering, as more load is applied to the transfer box or differential(s).

Ignoring these noises can result in a transfer box or differential failure that could be very costly. It's recommended that you have the vehicle checked by a 4x4 specialist as soon as possible.

If you have recently had tyres changed and the noise has become louder, there is a chance that this could be why, as some tyres are noisier than others.

13.3 Changing tyres on 4x4 vehicles

Certain transfer boxes and differentials on 4x4 systems are very prone to excessive wear caused by different tyre diameters. This is more common on vehicles fitted with constant four-wheel drive (4WD) or all-wheel drive (AWD).

Letting the front tyres on the car wear more than the rears can cause excessive wear on the 4WD components, and can result in a very costly failure. This can also occur if you replace just one worn tyre with a brand new one. Cars fitted with a central differential are very prone to this type of problem, which is why the manufacturers of these vehicles state that all four tyres should be changed at the same time. Failure to do so will eventually cause the 4WD system to fail, meaning that avoidable expensive repair or replacement will be necessary.

Tip Keep a close eye on the tyre

wear in order to avoid transfer box and differential problems. Regularly swapping the tyres around (front to back) will ensure that all four tyres receive a more even amount of wear, minimising the potential for damage to the 4WD system.

Tip Do not drive around constantly with the vehicle in 4WD if you have the option to switch to 2WD. You will not be helping to keep the tyre wear even, and will be prematurely wearing out the 4x4 system's components. Only use 4x4 mode when the weather or the driving surface requires it. This will help the system last longer.

13.4 Cannot engage four-wheel drive

If this is your first 4x4 or the first time you have tried using your 4x4, make sure you are trying to engage the 4x4 system in the correct manner. For example, certain vehicles can only be put into 4x4 when stationary, when in neutral, or when below a certain speed (say 25mph). The procedure for engaging 4x4 should be outlined in the user handbook.

If you have been looking after the 4x4 system, with regular inspections and oil changes, the problem is not likely to be an internal issue. It is more likely that the problem stems from the components that control the engaging

of the 4x4, such as the vacuum solenoid/system, electric actuator, ECU, fuses, and wiring.

If you engage the 4x4 system by pressing a switch or turning a dial on the dashboard, check that all of the relevant controls are working ok. The first thing to check is that none of the relevant fuses are blown (consult your handbook for fuse identity and location). If the vehicle has an electronic actuator to engage four-wheel drive, ensure that there is power going to it, so check that all of the fuses and associated wiring is working. Make sure you check the wiring that goes to the switch on the dashboard, as well as at the actuator end, on the transfer box/case underneath the car. If you have a fuse that keeps blowing, there is possibly a fault with the actuator, and it may need to be replaced.

On older vehicles, 4x4 may be engaged using a vacuum system. First check that all of the pipework to the vacuum actuator is in place and functioning correctly. Any loose pipework or lack of vacuum pressure will prevent the actuator from engaging four-wheel drive.

If you cannot easily identify the reason why the 4x4 is not engaging, the vehicle may need a professional diagnostic check to identify the fault codes being generated by the vehicle's electronic control units.

fourteen
Suspension, wheels & tyres

14.1 Loud banging noise from front on rough ground

This kind of noise will be related to a worn or broken suspension component that will need to be replaced.

The most likely cause is worn anti-roll bar drop links. These are the bars that connect the anti-roll bar to the suspension arm to reduce body roll. When the bushes at each end wear out, they will make a banging sound, especially when you are travelling over speed bumps or hit a pothole. These bushes are relatively cheap and easy to change and should be available from your local car parts shop.

Change these parts first, and also have the rest of the suspension components inspected for wear. If you are going to let a garage do the work, then perhaps you could have the mechanic confirm exactly what the fault is first.

A typical suspension drop link. When worn this can cause banging over bumps.

Can I still drive the car?

Yes, if an anti-roll bar drop link bush has failed, it will still be in position but will not be working correctly due to wear. Note the handling will not be at its best until the part has been replaced, and that other suspension parts and tyres will be exposed to higher forces, causing excessive wear (especially on the tyres).

14.2 Steering pulling to the left or right (not under braking)

If, when driving, you notice that the car is pulling to one side instead of straight ahead, there are a number of possible causes:
• Poorly matched tyre pressures. Even a small amount of difference between tyre pressures of the front two wheels can cause the car to pull to one side. Check that all of the tyres have the correct amount of pressure in them as per the manufacturer's recommendations.
• Poor wheel alignment. If the wheels are not correctly aligned in relation to each other and the car, pulling and excessive tyre wear can result. Possible causes are hitting a kerb resulting in suspension damage, a badly repaired vehicle or worn out suspension/steering components. Take the car to a wheel alignment specialist (usually found in tyre and exhaust centres) which will check and adjust alignment of the wheels. You may also receive advice about any worn parts that are causing the misalignment.
• Brake binding. A brake caliper that is not releasing correctly will cause the brake pads on one side to always be in contact with the brake disc. This will result in slight pulling to the side of the binding brake. A quick check for this, after a drive, is to compare the temperature of each wheel to see if

the one you feel is dragging is getting hotter than its opposite number. Have this problem investigated before it gets worse and causes a warped brake disc. The mechanic may repair or replace the faulty caliper.

14.3 Nail/debris stuck in tyre

If you know that you have a nail or something else relatively small stuck in a tyre, you will need to get the puncture fixed or the tyre replaced. If you do have to drive the vehicle to a garage with that tyre on it, do not take the object out of the tyre as it will probably be plugging the puncture or at least slowing down the leak.

Caution! Drive carefully in case the tyre suddenly deflates.

Nail stuck in tyre. Can be left in place until tyre is repaired or replaced.

Consider using an emergency puncture repair product until the tyre is repaired/replaced.

Tip You can use emergency puncture repair foam as a temporary fix to inflate the tyre until you can get the puncture repaired or the tyre replaced. These products are readily available from most car parts shops and many fuel filling stations: a useful item to carry in the car in case of a puncture. Note that these products work best where a straightforward puncture has occurred, eg a nail in the tread. If you have driven on the flat tyre for any distance or there is damage to the sidewalls, the product cannot be used.

14.4 Uneven tyre wear

The tyre treads should wear at an even rate across their width, so if you notice more wear in different places, look into this further.

How deep is this cut across the tyre tread? Have it checked at a tyre fitting centre.

Tyre worn more on outer edge is a reliable indicator of suspension problems.

This tyre is splitting, likely caused by age or poor suspension geometry: it needs urgent replacement.

The first thing to check is that the tyre is inflated sufficiently. An over-inflated tyre will experience more tread wear in the centre of its tread. An under-inflated tyre will experience more tread at the outside edges.

If you see high tread wear on one edge, this is an indication that there is a wheel alignment problem, and, possibly, worn suspension components. You will need to take the car to a wheel alignment specialist (at tyre and exhaust centres) which will check and adjust the alignment of the wheels. You will also receive advice about any worn parts that are causing the misalignment.

A tyre that does not make correct contact with the ground cannot provide its full level of grip. It is important to have the necessary alignment adjustments made and to change any worn suspension/steering parts.

14.5 Tyre will not inflate

If you cannot get any air into the tyre when you are trying to inflate it, the tyre valve is faulty and will need to be replaced. You will need to take the car to your local tyre and exhaust centre and ask them to change the valve for you. This will involve taking the tyre off the wheel, so there will be a labour charge on top of the cost of the new valve.

Can I still drive the car?

This will depend on how flat the tyre is. If there is very little air in it, you will be committing a driving offence as well as causing further damage to the tyre, which may result in it needing to be changed. Better to fit your car's spare

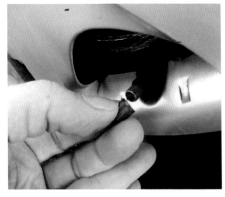

If the tyre will not inflate, it may have a faulty valve that will need to be replaced.

wheel (if it has one) and then have the faulty valve replaced.

If the tyre seems to be okay, and just needs topping up with air, it should be okay to drive to the tyre and exhaust centre to have a new valve fitted.

14.6 Bulging or uneven shaping of the tyre treads or walls

Mis-shaping of the tyre wall, like a bubble forming, is telling you that the tyre has a serious defect and at risk of suffering a blowout. Fit your spare wheel as soon as possible and have the tyre changed. The tyre can no longer be used and must be scrapped.

This kind of fault is usually caused by excessive force being applied to the tyre, such as hitting a kerb or driving over a brick. The sidewall of the tyre is damaged and weakened due to the impact, and will start to bulge at this weak spot.

Can I still drive the car?
No, you must not drive the car with this tyre on it, as there is risk of a

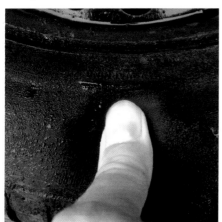

A soft spot in the tyre wall means the tyre is damaged internally. It can begin to bulge outwards. New tyre needed.

blowout that could result in a very serious accident. Fit the spare wheel straight away, and get the defective tyre replaced at a tyre and exhaust centre.

14.7 Wheel bolt seized

If you need to remove a wheel but one of the bolts will not loosen, try a different wheel brace from the one originally supplied with the car, as they can be very small. Using a larger wheel brace, or socket and tommy bar will allow more force to be applied to the wheel bolt and may loosen it. It will also make loosening the other wheel bolts much easier. Longer wheel braces can be purchased from most car parts shops.

If the bolt is still stuck, consider using a spray penetrant such as WD40. You may need to apply it a few times and let it work its way in. Take care not to get any of the lubricant onto the brake pads or brake discs.

Hitting the bolt a few times with a heavy hammer can help to loosen a tough wheel bolt. The air guns used at garages are also referred to as impact guns, because they have both a hammering and rotating action.

Take your car to a garage or tyre repair centre and ask the staff if they will loosen a seized bolt. The powerful equipment they have may work it loose. Also, they may be able to apply some heat to a really stubborn wheel bolt (not always possible with alloy wheels).

If you have breakdown cover and the wheel needs to come off because you have a puncture, give your service provider a call, as this situation should be covered by your policy.

Take care not to apply too much force when removing a wheel bolt. They can only take so much force and, if you are using things like scaffold poles to apply more force, you are at serious risk

Wheel bolts can become seized over time due to age, excessive heat, corrosion, etc.

Try using a longer tool to unfasten a tight or seized wheel bolt.

of the wheel bolt snapping, which will be a repair job for a garage.

If you do manage to get the wheel bolt removed, consider replacing it with a new one so that the problem does not happen again.

Caution! Don't apply grease to the wheel bolts.

_____

14.8 Wheel bolt broken
_____

Broken wheel bolts often occur as a result of them being overtightened when the wheels are refitted.

Wheel bolts are designed to shear off below the tapered part, just leaving the straight threaded section in the wheel hub. This means that removing the other wheel bolts will still allow you to take the wheel off the car, to see if you can remove the remainder of the bolt.

You may be able to grab the remaining thread to remove it. If it is too tight or there is not enough to grab on to, you may need to use a stud extractor. This involves drilling a small hole into the end of the broken bolt and

Try spray penetrant like WD40 on tough bolts, but don't get any on the brakes.

Tap the wheel bolt with a heavy hammer to help loosen it. (Courtesy CarBasics.co.uk)

screwing in a suitably sized extractor. These are threaded anti-clockwise, so as you turn it and it tightens into the drilled hole, it should allow you to unscrew the bolt. If you are unable to remove the remaining thread, you will need to have it removed at a garage.

Can I still drive the car?
The car has been designed with a specific number of wheel bolts, usually four or five. Driving with fewer will put more strain onto the remaining bolts.

However, if you really do need to drive the car to the garage to be repaired, and you are missing just one bolt, you should only travel a short distance.

Caution! Drive slowly (avoid fast roads), especially around corners, apply the brakes gently, and accelerate slowly. If you experience a wheel wobble or change in driving feel, stop the car immediately and do not proceed any further.

14.9 Locking wheel nuts/bolts

If you vehicle is fitted with alloy wheels, there is a possibility they will be fitted with locking wheels nuts to prevent them being stolen.

Locking wheel nuts or bolts need a special fitting (key) to allow them to be removed from the car, and if this is lost or broken then you will not be able to remove the wheels.

Always keep the key somewhere safe inside the car, in case of a puncture. However, if your key gets lost or damaged, there are a number of options available to you:

• Buy replacement key – if you have any details about the locking wheel nuts, such as who manufactured it, original packaging, part numbers etc, you may be able to source a replacement.
• Locking wheel nut removers – these can be purchased from motor factors and online, and are designed with a deep reverse thread that should grip the outside of the nut and unfasten it. Note that these do not always work successfully, and will also render the wheel bolt unusable once it has been removed, meaning that you will have to source a replacement.
• Local tyre fitters – your local tyre fitter may be able to help you remove the locking nut, as it is probably a problem they experience on a regular basis. Some carry generic keys that can be used to remove many locking wheel nuts, so one may fit yours.
• Breakdown service – in the event of a puncture where the locking wheel nut prevents you from fitting a replacement, your breakdown service may be able to attend and remove the locking wheel nut.

Typical locking wheel nuts.

fifteen
Engine coolant

15.1 Very little coolant in the engine

Caution! If the engine is hot be careful not to burn yourself by touching components. There may be a spray of scalding steam when the system filler cap is removed: cover it with a heavy cloth as you remove it, or wait until everything cools down.

However much water is needed to refill the system to the correct level will indicate how much coolant has been lost.

Once you have filled up the coolant system, check for leaks before you start the engine. If no leaks are apparent, start the car and check for leaks again. Keep the engine running and take a few minutes to look all around the engine bay and underneath the car. If coolant is pouring out quickly from anywhere, it is important to stop the car straight away.

If the car has a slow coolant leak and you have a journey to continue, you must proceed with caution. Keep a close eye on the temperature gauge and also the car's interior heating system (see tips). You will probably have to stop regularly to top up the coolant until you reach your destination or a garage.

Tip Keep a close eye on the engine temperature gauge. As the water in the coolant system gets lower, the remaining water will get hotter quicker, so as soon as the gauge needle nears the danger zone you must stop the car straight away.

Tip Only in an emergency! Turn on the interior heater and have it blowing hot air; use this as an indicator, as whilst it is blowing hot, it shows that there is still water in the cooling system. As soon as it blows cooler you must stop the car immediately.

See the next section for advice on how to perform a leak repair.

Top up the cooling system with the correct amount of anti-freeze/summer coolant.

If you know that your car has suffered a loss of engine coolant, and know that the engine has recently overheated, consider the likelihood that the engine will be damaged. Most commonly this will be in the form of a blown cylinder head gasket or a warped cylinder head. See sections 5.3 and 6.1 for further information.

15.2 Coolant leaking

The first thing you should do is stop the car and turn off the engine. Check the coolant level by observing the expansion tank – the level should be between the 'min' and 'max' markings. It is important to turn the engine off as soon as possible to avoid potential serious damage.

See the caution note in 15.1. Top up the coolant if necessary, then restart the engine. Look for steam or water coming from any hoses or from the radiator. Also, check the ground under the engine to see if there is anything dripping from above.

The type of repair needed will depend on where the leak is coming from:

• Leak coming from the radiator. You can use stop-leak treatment to plug it. Many stop-leak treatments are sold as 'permanent,' and therefore the radiator should not need replacing/repair. However, after any type of coolant system repair always keep a close eye on the coolant levels.

• Leak coming from hose. You can easily use repair tape to fix it temporarily.

Check under the car for signs of coolant leaks. (Courtesy CarBasics.co.uk)

These repair tapes can be purchased from most car parts shops and some filling stations. These self-amalgamating tapes should only be treated as a temporary repair, and you should get the faulty hose replaced as soon as possible. Note that Holts RadWeld does state that it can repair hose leaks as well as radiator leaks.

Both of these leak repair products are relatively cheap and easy to use. They can get you out of an emergency, and can be found at your local car parts shops. Even garages and supermarkets carry them in stock.

Can I still drive the car?
With a slow leak and a constant eye on engine temperature and water levels, you should be able to drive until the leak has been fixed. Carry a large bottle of water in case you need to top up.

Read the tips in section 15.1 to help keep the engine temperature down.

Remember, if you've temporarily topped up the system with a substantial amount of water, it will have to be drained and the diluted coolant replaced with the correct water/anti-freeze-inhibitor mixture as soon as possible, especially in winter.

sixteen

Fuel

16.1 Running out of fuel

We have all tried to get more miles out of our car than the fuel in our tanks may allow, which is why it is always important to carry a spare fuel can, so you have an emergency supply should you run out. If you don't own a spare can and do run out, the nearest garage should be able to sell you one that you can then fill up. Take it back to the car and refuel, and, hopefully, the car should start. Running out of fuel on modern cars can be very problematic, and is something that should always be avoided.

The process of getting fuel from the tank and into the fuelling system once air has entered the system is called purging. Most modern cars should be self-purging, and able to restart after running out of fuel. But please note that it may take some time to restart the car as it tries to pump the fuel from the tank into the engine. It is important here to have a fully charged and healthy battery.

Older vehicles may have to be manually purged, and you will need to check the user or workshop manual for instructions. This normally involves operating a plunger in the engine bay to draw the fuel through from the tank.

If you have an old or partially charged battery, there is a strong chance that the battery will run flat before enough fuel is pumped through to the engine.

If the car feels hesitant or splutters after running out of fuel, consider changing the fuel filters or having the fuel-injectors cleaned. The fault may be due to these parts getting clogged up because you ran the car so low on fuel that debris from the bottom of the tank has been introduced to the fuelling system.

16.2 Filling up with the wrong fuel

This happens to over 150,000 UK drivers each year, so you're not alone.

Caution! The most important thing is: do **not** to turn on the ignition and do not to start the car. This is critical, because as soon as you start the car, you will transfer fuel into the engine. We are not talking about a bit of damage – it could be catastrophic!

The RAC has a special service called RAC Fuel Patrol, which will drain the fuel tank at the roadside, flush out the fuel system, and provide you with enough fuel to get you on your way. You do not need to be a member to use this service.

What to do if I did start my car?
The car probably stopped of its own accord and then you realised what you had done. Do not try to restart the car, as you will just be pumping more of the wrong fuel into the engine and causing more damage to it.

What you must now do is arrange with a breakdown service or garage to come and collect the car so it can be assessed for damage and repaired.

Important! Check your vehicle insurance – there is a small possibility that damage caused by misfueling may be covered. Your insurance policy may exclude damage caused by misfueling especially with third-party only cover, but it is definitely worth checking out.

16.3 Strong smell of fuel

On modern vehicles with fuel-injected engines you should never be able to smell petrol or diesel unless there is a fault. If you drive an older vehicle

Inspecting fuel lines and fuel-injector connections for fuel leaks because of a strong smell.

that has carburettors or a manual choke, petrol smells are probably quite common and not necessarily an indicator of a significant problem.

The fuel systems on modern vehicles are sealed and there should be no smell of the fuel inside them.

A strong smell of diesel or petrol can be caused by such things as leaking fuel lines, hose connectors, fuel-injector leaks or pressure problems or even poor ignition timing.

Whatever the cause, chances are that it is pretty serious and requires the attention of an expert mechanic. It is not something that you should hope will be okay, and not something you should just clean up and carry on with your journey.

Caution! Turn the car engine off, take the keys out of the ignition and do not use any of the vehicle electrics.

Can I still drive the car?
Until you have identified what the problem is and fixed it, you shouldn't drive the car. Any fuel that is leaking has the potential to catch fire and cause a potentially fatal incident.

Caution! Never loosen, unfasten or retighten any components of your vehicle's fuelling system yourself. This kind of work must only ever be undertaken by a qualified mechanic.

16.4 Fuel filler flap won't open

If the fuel filler flap won't open, it is possibly because the lock has not released.

If the flap does have a key-operated lock on it, and it has always been unlocked when you've filled up in the past, then you clearly have a flap controlled by the central locking system.

Some vehicles have a specific button that has to be pressed to release the fuel filler flap.

These lockable flaps should have a method for manually overriding and opening the flap from inside the car. You will need to refer to the car's user handbook to find the specific method for your vehicle.

Here is a non-car specific method that may help if you do not have a user handbook. Gain access to the fuel filler flap mechanism, which is located inside the car. Remove the interior trim panel that is behind the fuel filler, and you should be able to see the filler flap mechanism. You should see a rod or lever, which will operate the locking pin on the other side. Using a screwdriver or long nose pliers, manually pull/push the rod so that it disengages the locking pin. When you have done this, the fuel flap should be released.

Getting it open solves the immediate problem of getting fuel into the tank. However, you will need to ascertain the cause to prevent the problem from happening again. The fault will probably be a blown fuse, faulty switch, sticking lock, faulty solenoid, or faulty wiring.

Tip You can also use this method if your car has a flat battery or the central locking has failed.

Tip If you have noticed that the fuel flap won't unlock when the weather is very cold, it may be that the lock is freezing up. To help stop this, open the fuel filler flap and spray some WD40 or other spray penetrant/lubricant into the lock/pin mechanism, thus lubricating it and dispersing any water that could freeze again.

seventeen

Winter

As far as winter problems with cars are concerned, prevention is always better than cure. This chapter outlines a few tips that should help keep you motoring during the winter months.

17.1 Frozen locks

If the temperature drops overnight, you can find yourself in a rush to get to work only to find that you cannot get into your car because the door locks have frozen.

You probably already know that a spray of de-icer or a warmed up door key will help you to get into the car. If you do not have any de-icer to hand, you can use a hand sanitiser that contains alcohol. Spread some onto your key and try to get it into the lock; the alcohol should start to melt the ice.

Preventing frozen door locks
One good way of preventing frozen door locks, other than keeping your car in the garage, is to spray WD40 into the

Frozen door locks can be a real nuisance.

locks. WD40 is not only a lubricant, but also a water dispersant, which will help to prevent freezing. This is easier if you use the spray tube that comes with the WD40 as you can push it past the flap that seals the key hole.

Tip Keep a spare can of de-icer in the house as well as in the car, in case

Spray lubricant into the locks to prevent freezing in winter.

you return the can to the house after using it.

If you manage to unlock the car and find that you cannot pull open the door, this is probably because it has frozen solid. Don't keep pulling on the door handle, as you may cause damage to it, the door panel or the door's seals.

Frozen doors are often caused by rain getting into the gaps around the door, then freezing solid.

Try to avoid chipping away at the ice around the door with a scraper, as you may scratch the paintwork. Instead spray de-icer onto the area to melt it.

Preventing frozen doors
To prevent the door seals from freezing to the body, open the doors and spread a little petroleum jelly onto the rubber seals that run all around them. This should prevent any water/moisture freezing the seals together. You will need to take a little caution when entering the

the locks freeze. You will also find that the de-icer kept in the house will spray better than one that is really cold from being in the car. Just make sure that

Petroleum jelly on door seals can stop doors from freezing shut.

car so as to not get any jelly on your clothes, but at least you should be able to actually get into it.

17.3 Frozen windscreen wipers

NEVER use the windscreen wipers to remove anything from the windscreen other than rain until you have checked that the wiper blades are not stuck to the window. Even then, using the wipers to shift a lot of snow from the windscreen is going to put excessive wear on the wiper motor and mechanism, and you are at risk of breaking it or blowing a fuse.

If you can hear the windscreen wiper motors turning but the wipers are not moving, you will have damaged a part of the windscreen wiper mechanism, and it will most likely need to be replaced. The chances are that something has bent or sheared off,

and it will not be just a case of bolting it back together.

If the wipers are not working and you can't hear the motor, you've probably blown the fuse and it will need to be replaced. Check the car's user handbook for the fuse position.

Tip Before you try lifting the wiper blades from the windscreen, give them a spray with de-icer in case they are frozen in place. This should prevent damage to the wiper blades.

Tip Before operating the windscreen wipers, make sure that all the built-up snow and ice around the wiper arms is removed, especially where the arms meet the body. Failure to do so may cause damage to the wiper motor or wiper mechanism under the bonnet.

Avoid damage to wiper blades and motors by removing all ice and snow from around them.

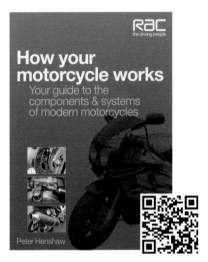
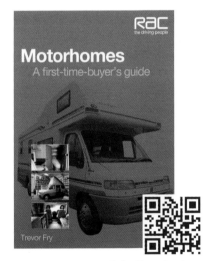

Simple fixes for your car
How to do small jobs yourself and save money

Carl Collins

ISBN: 978-1-845845-18-6 • Paperback
21x14.8cm • £9.99* UK/$19.95* USA
80 pages • 82 colour pictures

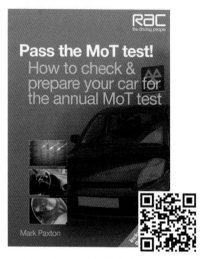

Pass the MoT test!
How to check & prepare your car for the annual MoT test

Mark Paxton

ISBN: 978-1-845844-74-5 • Paperback
21x14.8cm • £9.99* UK/$19.95* USA
80 pages • 99 colour pictures

Selling your car
How to make your car look great and sell it faster

Nigel Knight

ISBN: 978-1-845844-50-9 • Paperback
21x14.8cm • £9.99* UK/$19.95* USA
96 pages • 136 colour pictures

The Essential Driver's Handbook
What to do in the event of an accident, roadside first-aid, safety tips for lone drivers & much more

Bruce Grant

ISBN: 978-1-845845-32-2 • Paperback
21x14.8cm • £9.99* UK/$19.95* USA
80 pages • 100 pictures

For more info on Veloce titles, visit our website at www.veloce.co.uk
email: info@veloce.co.uk • Tel: +44(0)1305 260068
* prices subject to change, p&p extra

ISBN: 978-1-845843-96-0 • Paperback
21x14.8cm • £9.99* UK/$19.95* USA
96 pages • 177 colour pictures

ISBN: 978-1-845843-88-5 • Paperback
21x14.8cm • £9.99* UK/$19.95* USA
80 pages • 115 colour pictures

ISBN: 978-1-845840-95-2 • Paperback
21x14.8cm • £9.99* UK/$19.95* USA
80 pages • 89 colour pictures

ISBN: 978-1-845844-77-6 • Paperback
21x14.8cm • £6.99* UK/$11.99* USA
64 pages • 97 colour pictures

For more info on Veloce titles, visit our website at www.veloce.co.uk
email: info@veloce.co.uk • Tel: +44(0)1305 260068
* prices subject to change, p&p extra

ISBN: 978-1-845843-10-6 • Paperback
21x14.8cm • £12.99* UK/$24.95* USA
128 pages • 67 colour and b&w pictures

ISBN: 978-1-845843-51-9 • Paperback
21x14.8cm • £9.99* UK/$19.95* USA
96 pages • 32 colour pictures

ISBN: 978-1-845841-02-7 • Paperback
15x10.5cm • £4.99* UK/$9.95* USA
208 pages • 200 colour pictures

ISBN: 978-1-845843-79-3 • Paperback
21x14.8cm • £9.99* UK/$19.95* USA
80 pages • 90 colour pictures

For more info on Veloce titles, visit our website at www.veloce.co.uk
email: info@veloce.co.uk • Tel: +44(0)1305 260068
* prices subject to change, p&p extra

Index